teach yourself...
C++

AL STEVENS

MIS:
PRESS

A Subsidiary of
Henry Holt and Co., Inc.

Third Edition—1993

ISBN Book 1-55828-250-5

Printed in the United States of America

10 9 8 7 6 5 4 3 2 1

MIS:Press books are available at special discounts for bulk purchases for sales promotions, premiums, fund-raising, or educational use. Special editions or book excerpts can also be created to specification.

For details contact:

      Special Sales Director
      MIS:Press
      a subsidiary of Henry Holt and Company, Inc.
      115 West 18th Street
      New York, New York 10011

Development Editor: Margot Owens Pagan

Copy Editor: Suzanne Ingrao

DEDICATION

To the fond memory of Joseph Jensen Stevens

ACKNOWLEDGEMENTS

Thanks first to the following vendors for their contributions of C++ compiler products:

Borland International

Comeau Computing

Microsoft Corporation

Symantec Corporation

A special thanks to Greg Comeau for his comments on earlier editions of this book which contributed significantly to the improvement of this third edition.

Thanks, also, to the readers of my column in Dr. Dobb's Journal. Your support and encouragement make writing about programming the most rewarding and fulfilling of tasks.

Finally, thanks to Bjarne Stroustrup for creating C++.

Contents

Preface

This book is the third edition of *teach yourself C++*, a tutorial text with which you, a C programmer, can teach yourself C++. The first edition was published in 1990, and the second edition was published in 1991. Several significant changes have occurred in the C++ language and community since then. AT&T's Version 3.0 has become the targeted version for compiler developers. Many new C++ programming environments have emerged, including several that run in the MS-DOS environment. The ANSI X3J16 committee is well underway toward a standard definition of C++. The major addition that version 3.0 adds to the language is *templates*, formerly called *parameterized data* types. The formal definition is now addressing the feature called *exception handling*, and this book describes how that feature will work in future implementations.

You will learn C++ in this book the same way thousands of C programmers did with the first two editions—in the same sequence that I learned C++ before I wrote the first book, except that you will have help. I waded through a lot of heavy stuff when I first set out to learn C++. From that experience, I developed what I believe to be the correct sequence of learning steps that a C programmer must take to learn and use the features of C++.

Most of the exercises in this book will compile and run with version 3.0 or higher implementation of C++. I have compiled them with Borland C++ 3.1, Comeau C++ 3.0, Microsoft C++ 7.0, and Zortech C++ 3.1. Note that the compilers' version numbers do not always align with AT&T's but rather with the evolution of those products as C and C++ development environments.

The exercises in Chapter 11 on templates work only with Borland C++, Comeau C++ and Zortech C++, because these compilers have implemented templates. The exercises in Chapter 12 on exception handling do not compile with any of the compilers, because none of them have implemented exception handling yet. Microsoft C++ uses macro substitutions that resemble exception handling, but the syntax does not comply with the AT&T definition. A C++ compiler that implements exceptions is expected from Watcom, another compiler vendor, by the time this book is available. Use Chapter 12 as a guide to how exceptions should work once they are implemented. None of the exercises in any of the chapters are specific to the PC/AT platform or to any particular compiler's extensions to the language, libraries, or classes.

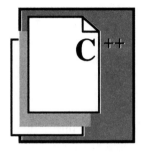

Introduction

This book enables you, as a C programmer, to teach yourself the C++ programming language. C++ is a superset of the C language, containing most of the program constructs of C, so the C programmer already has a head start on the learning process. The C++ language adds extensions to C that improve its syntax, expand its application, and bring to it some of the features of object-oriented programming.

teach yourself C++ leads you through the learning process with a series of exercises. Each exercise includes C++ source code that you can compile and execute. To get the maximum benefit from these lessons, you should have a programmer's editor and a C++ compiler with which to practice.

The C++ exercises in this book lead you through the subjects related to C++ in a sequence that introduces simpler concepts first, and then uses them in subsequent exercises where gradually more complex subjects are developed. These exercises often build upon the ones that precede them, and you frequently modify programs that you built in earlier exercises. Therefore, it is important that you follow the exercises in the order in which they appear. This book is a tutorial designed to help you teach the C++ programming language to yourself. *It is not a language reference manual.*

A complex subject such as a programming language often requires you to go into a learning loop. You cannot learn a lesson without knowing about a prerequisite lesson, which itself has the new lesson as a prerequisite. A case in point is the C++ standard input/output streams. To fully comprehend their syntax, you must know about C++ classes and overloaded operators, both of which are advanced topics in the hallowed halls of C++ learning. Yet to progress to where you can learn those advanced topics, you need to walk through an orderly sequence of program exercises that use the keyboard and screen, devices that are in the exclusive domain of input/output streams. What choice do you have but to use the **cin** and **cout** objects of the **istream** and **ostream** classes with a blind acceptance that what they do will eventually make sense? Trust the book and be patient—everything eventually becomes clear. Stick with it, and you will be rewarded.

Because of this circular approach, the programmer who is already well versed in C++ might well find things to criticize in this book. Some exercises do not include code constructs that a seasoned C++ programmer would recognize as conventional, appropriate, or even downright necessary. These omissions are intentional and are because of the sequence of learning that is built into *teach yourself C++*. Eventually the book covers those bases. Other omissions are due to the highly advanced nature of C++ and the kind of strange and exotic code that it permits. There are elements in C++, just as in C, that a tutorial work should spare the newcomer. Later, when you have the language well in hand, you can push it to its limits.

The exercise programs in *teach yourself C++* are small. They do not pretend to be full-blown, useful programs that you take out into the workplace. The purpose of each exercise is to demonstrate the behavior of a particular feature of C++. Some of the exercises have the potential to grow into useful software tools, and you should view all of them with this possibility in mind. The strength of extensible programming languages such as C and C++ lies in their potential for the programmer to build reusable software tools. You will soon learn that C++, far more than C and most other traditional programming languages, readily adapts itself to that potential.

Most exercises in this book are complete programs that you can compile and execute. A few exercises illustrate common programming errors and might not compile or run properly. Where this is true, the book and the comments in the code clearly point it out. Some programs consist of the combined code from several exercises. Where this happens, the dependent code always follows closely behind the code it needs. You will have no trouble keeping track of where you are if you follow the exercises in the order in which they appear.

A Brief History of C++

The C++ programming language was designed and originally developed by Bjarne Stroustrup in the Computer Science Research Center at AT&T Bell Labs in Murray Hill, New Jersey. He began this work in about 1980 in answer to a need for a simulation language that had the features of object-oriented programming, then a relatively new programming paradigm. Rather than design a new language from the ground up, Dr. Stroustrup decided to add the features he wanted to the well-established C language, itself an earlier development from within the Center.

C was already implemented on several different architectures, and it already had the property of supporting portable-program development, so Dr. Stroustrup made an historic decision: He elected to develop the C++ language system as a translator program that compiles C++ source language into C source language. The translated C source language could then be compiled on any computer system that supports C. He called his translator program CFRONT, and many implementations of C++ have been ports of that same CFRONT program and its successors, the source code of which is available to language system developers under license from AT&T. The C++ language has been available outside of AT&T since about 1985.

Over the years, C++ has continued through several versions, with the latest being version 3.0. Dr. Stroustrup remains its staunchest advocate and is a strong contributing presence wherever C++ issues surface. With the standardization of C now completed by the ANSI X3J11 committee, a new committee, X3J16, was formed to tackle the formidable task of defining a standard for C++.

The C++ Legacy to C Programmers

Even if you have never seen a C++ program, you have been touched by it. Although C came before C++, many of the features in C today saw their first light of day in the improvements that Dr. Stroustrup sought to add to the language when he defined his superset. These features were widely admired, were incorporated into various C compilers, and were ultimately adopted by the ANSI X3J11 committee as parts of standard C.

Examples of the C++ improvements that are now standard in C are function prototypes, void, and the const type-specifier.

Learning C++

C++, like C before it, is becoming the language of choice among programmers. Since the first edition of this book came out, C++ language systems have appeared in every environment and on most architectures where C once reigned supreme, adding testimony to the assertion of Dr. Stroustrup and others that C++ will ultimately replace C. It therefore behooves the rest of us to learn this new technique.

The best way for a C programmer to learn C++ is to take it a small step at a time, trying its various features in a sequence that introduces small portions of the C++ extensions. Remember, with a C++ compiler, you can still build a C program. The full range of C language features and C standard-library functions is automatically a part of every C++ language system because C++, as originally designed, compiled C++ code into C code that passed through to a C compiler. So you can begin with the C that you already know and gradually add the enhancements of C++, learning a little bit at a time.

The Organization of this Book

Chapters 1 through 12 are the lessons and exercises that you use to teach yourself C++. The lessons begin with an elementary introduction to the extensions that C++ brings to C and proceed through to the more complex features of the language.

Chapter 13 is an introduction to object-oriented programming. Its purpose is to allow you to relate your new knowledge of C++ to the terms and concepts of object-oriented technology.

A glossary and bibliography follow Chapter 13. The glossary provides brief definitions of terms that are common to C++. The bibliography lists the books and articles that contributed to the research that went into this book. As such, it constitutes a reasonable library for the C++ programmer.

The C++ programming language operates in many environments on many platforms. Some of the implementations are ports of the AT&T CFRONT translator program; others are complete compiler systems with integrated editors, debuggers, and linkers. To avoid confusion, this book refers to all such implementations as C++ compilers.

Chapter

1

C++ Basics

C++ is a superset of the C language with extensions and improvements. Extensions are new features in the language; while improvements are better ways of doing the things that C already does. You will teach yourself C++ first by gathering those improvements and extensions as additions to what you can already do as a C programmer. Later, you will apply this new knowledge as you learn, step by step, the development of systems that employ the object-oriented features of C++. This chapter is your first step toward that goal. You will learn about:

- The **iostream** class
- C++ comments
- Function prototypes
- Keywords

The First C++ Programs

Exercise 1.1 is the first C++ program for you to consider.

```
main()
{
}
```

Exercise 1.1 The Simplest C++ Program.

Look familiar? It should. It's the smallest possible C program as well. Because C++ is a superset of the C language, you can use a C++ compiler to develop and compile C programs. The minimum program just shown does not do anything, of course. It contains no more than one function, which, as in C, must be named **main**. Exercise 1.2 is a program that does something.

 The exercises in this book declare the **main** function with no return type, which implies that **main** returns an integer; yet the **main** functions in the exercises have no **return** statement and, therefore, return nothing. The C++ language specification says that the **main** function type is implementation dependent. Traditionally **main** returns an integer value, which the program returns to the system. If **main** returns no value, the compiler assumes a **void** return, and the system receives an undefined return value when the program terminates by a return from **main**. Most C++ text books declare **main** the same way this one does. Most C++ compilers issue the warning. The Zortech C++ compiler issues an error and refuses to compile programs with **main** functions that are declared to return something but that do not return anything. This compiler behavior is unconventional. If you are using the Zortech compiler and compiling the exercises one at a time, either add the **void** return type to all **main** functions or insert a statement at the end of the **main** function that returns a zero value. The batch files on the companion diskette that build all exercises with the Zortech compiler include macros to compensate for the unconventional compiler behavior.

```
#include <iostream.h>

main()
{
    cout << "Hello, world";
}
```

Exercise 1.2 Hello.cpp.

This program is *hello.cpp*, the C++ equivalent to the *hello.c* program that introduced the world to the C language in Kernighan and Ritchie's *The C Programming Language*. But instead of *stdio.h*, this program includes *iostream.h*, and instead of a **printf** call, it uses an unfamiliar syntax with the undefined variable name **cout**, the bitwise shift left operator (<<), and, the only familiar part of the example, a literal string expression that greets the world. You might well wonder about the meaning of it all.

Input/Output Streams

The *hello.cpp* program in Exercise 1.2 is your introduction to the powerful C++ facility called the **class**, a feature that lets a programmer define new data types and operators. A complete explanation of the class is premature in this chapter, but you should know that C++ compiler products use classes to implement an improved stream input/output system. That design is a standard in C++ programs, and because you will be using these improved streams to read display information throughout these lessons, and you need this early exposure to it.

The Standard Output Stream

The **cout** variable, seen in Exercise 1.2, is the C++ standard output stream, which writes to the console:

```
cout << "Hello, world";
```

In exercise 1.2, the "Hello, world" string is sent to the standard output device stream. The << operator is the output operator. It points symbolically from what is being sent to where it is going. You can think of **cout**, **cin**, and **cerr** (described soon) as devices that are like *stdout, stdin,* and *stderr* in C programs. In fact, these identifiers name objects—instances—of classes. In this example, the string is going to the **cout** object.

Suppose you wanted to display the contents of an integer variable on the screen. In C you would use the **printf** function along with a format string that describes the parameters to **printf** like the following:

```
printf("%d", amount);
```

Exercise 1.3 sends data values to the C++ stream output device directly—no format string is required.

```
#include <iostream.h>

main()
{
    int amount = 123;
    cout << amount;
}
```

Exercise 1.3 The Standard Output Stream.

Exercise 1.3 displays an integer value on the console. Suppose you want to display the value as part of a sentence. Using the techniques that you learned in Exercise 1.3, you can display different data types by sending each of them in turn to the output stream. The **cout** stream can discern the format of the data type from the variable's identifier because the C++ compiler makes the association when it compiles your code. The discussions in Chapters 4 and 8 on function and operator overloading show how the compiler does this. For now you can accept it as a feature of the standard output stream in C++. Ready or not, you must now acquaint yourself with **iostream** input and output, because you need them to enter and display data values.

Exercise 1.4 illustrates how to send a string, an integer, and a character constant to the output stream.

```
#include <iostream.h>

main()
{
    int amount = 123;
    cout << "The value of amount is ";
    cout << amount;
    cout << '.';
}
```

Exercise 1.4 Multiple Data Type to the Standard Output Stream.

Exercise 1.4 displays the following message on the screen:

```
The value of amount is 123.
```

The exercise sends three different data types to **cout**, a string literal, the integer **amount** variable, and a character-constant '.'. This approach might send you scurrying back to the standard C language **printf** function, because this exercise used three statements where **printf** could have done it in one.

Exercise 1.5 sends multiple data types to the standard output stream in one line of code. The exercise displays the same value as that in Exercise 1.4.

```
#include <iostream.h>

main()
{
    int amount = 123;
    cout << "The value of amount is " << amount << '.';
}
```

Exercise 1.5 Several Outputs in One Statement.

Exercise 1.5 connects several data types with the << operator. This behavior is a by-product of the **this** pointer (which is used in the definition of the stream class and that gets full treatment in Chapter 7). For now, accept the behavior and forge ahead.

Formatted Output

The ways that you have used **cout** so far do not apply the well-formatted displays of the C **printf** family of functions. Suppose you want to display the hexadecimal representation of a variable for example. The C **printf** function handles that nicely. How does C++ do it?

The iostream system associates a set of manipulators with the output stream. These manipulators change the displayed numerical base for integer arguments. You insert the manipulators into the stream to make the change. The manipulators' symbolic names are **dec**, **oct**, and **hex**.

Exercise 1.6 uses manipulators to display an integer in three numerical base representations.

```
#include <iostream.h>

main()
{
    int amount = 123;
    cout << dec << amount << ' ' << oct << amount << ' '
        << hex << amount;
}
```

Exercise 1.6 Formatting Numerical Data.

The exercise inserts the manipulators, **dec**, **oct**, and **hex**, into the stream to convert the value that follows—**amount**—into different numerical base representations.

Exercise 1.6 displays the following result:

```
123 173 7b
```

Each of the values shown is the decimal value 123 in a different base representation.

The Standard Error Stream

The **cerr** object uses the same syntax as **cout**, with the exception that **cerr** sends its output to the standard error device. This technique allows you to display error messages on the console—even when the program's user redirects the standard output device.

The Standard Input Stream

Now that you can display all kinds of data on the screen, you will want to read some data into your programs as well. The **iostream** version of standard input is implemented by the **cin** object.

Exercise 1.7 uses **cin** to read an integer from the keyboard.

```
#include <iostream.h>

main()
{
    int amount;
    cout << "Enter an amount...";
    cin >> amount;
    cout << "The amount you entered was " << amount;
}
```

Exercise 1.7 The Standard Input Stream.

Exercise 1.7 sends a string to **cout** to prompt you for input. The **cin** device sends the value that you enter to the **amount** integer variable. The exercise then displays the amount variable on **cout** to demonstrate that the **cin** operation worked.

Exercise 1.7 displays the following messages. The first "123" is the amount you would type into the program.

```
Enter an amount...123
The amount you entered was 123
```

Suppose that you use this program in a system with a 16-bit integer (such as the PC). If you enter the value 65535, the program displays -1. If you enter 65536, the program displays 0. These displays occur because the amount variable is a signed integer. Change the **amount** variable's type to an unsigned integer and retry the program. Then see what happens if you enter a value that has decimal places.

Try entering alphabetic characters instead of numbers into Exercise 1.7. It doesn't work, does it? The **cin** device works with strings—*character arrays*—as well as numbers, but you must use the correct data type.

Exercise 1.8 uses the **cin** device to read a string value from the keyboard into a character array.

```cpp
#include <iostream.h>

main()
{
    char name[20];
    cout << "Enter a name...";
    cin >> name;
    cout << "The name you entered was " << name;
}
```

Exercise 1.8 Reading a String.

Exercise 1.8 displays the following messages. The name "Tyler" is used here for the name you would type into the program.

```
Enter a name...Tyler
The name you entered was Tyler
```

Exercise 1.8 has a flaw. The character array is only 20 characters long. If you type too many characters, the stack overflows and peculiar things happen. The **get** function solves this problem, and you will learn about **get** in Chapter 10, but for now the exercises assume that you will not type more characters than the declared character array can accept.

You should know that **cin** and **cout** are not part of the compiled C++ language as such. They are not built-in data types, and the << and >> operators are not, in this context, built-in C++ operators. The input and output streams are implemented as C++ classes, and **cin** and **cout** are global instances of those classes. This implementation exists outside the C++ compiler system itself, just as the **printf** and **scanf** functions are implemented through functions in the C language and not as a part of the C language. But where C limits its extensibility to function and structure definitions, C++ allows you to define new data types and to associate custom operators with those data types. You will learn how to do this later.

C++ Comments

The exercises so far have been short with no comments. C++ supports the standard C comment format. The /* character sequence begins a comment and the */ sequence ends it. But C++ has another comment format. The C++ comment token is the double-slash (//) sequence. Wherever this sequence appears (other than inside a string literal), everything to the end of the current line is a comment.

Exercise 1.9 repeats Exercise 1.8 and adds comments to the program.

```
#include <iostream.h>

main()
{
    char name[20];              // declare a name string
    cout << "Enter a name...";  // request a name
    cin >> name;                // read the name
    // ------------ display the name
    cout << "The name you entered was " << name;
}
```

Exercise 1.9 C++ Comments.

Prototypes

Standard C supports function-declaration blocks that describe the function's class, return value, and parameters to the C compiler. This feature, called the *function prototype*, allows the compiler to check the function's definition and function calls with the prototype. C compilers do not require function prototypes. If you provide prototypes, all references to the functions must comply with the prototypes; but if you omit them, the best that you can get are warning messages.

C++ requires that all functions have prototypes. To illustrate, Exercise 1.10 uses a function with no prototype to display the "Hello, world" message on the screen.

```
#include <iostream.h>

main()
{
    display("Hello, world");
}

void display(char *s)
{
    cout << s;
}
```

Exercise 1.10 A Program Without Function Prototypes.

Because the **display** function has no prototype, the program in Exercise 1.10 does not compile without error messages.

Exercise 1.11 adds a function prototype to the program in Exercise 1.10. This addition allows the program to compile without errors.

```
#include <iostream.h>

display(char *s);

main()
{
    display("Hello, world");
}

void display(char *s)
{
    cout << s;
}
```

Exercise 1.11 A Program with a Function Prototype.

Now, with a proper prototype, the program compiles and runs correctly. C++ also requires that the function definition declare the types of function parameters within the parentheses that follow the function's name as shown here.

```
void func(int x, int y)  // C++ function
{
    // ....
}
```

Standard C accepts this format, too, but still permits the old K&R style where parameter declarations are listed immediately below the function name as shown here.

```
func(x, y)  // K&R C function, invalid C++
int x;
int y;
{
    // ....
}
```

C++ uses stronger parameter type-checking than C, however, and therefore does not accept the older style.

The prototype and function-declaration requirements are strict but necessary ones. They are exceptions to the general rule that a C++ compiler can compile a C program. If your C programs do not have function prototypes and new-style function-declaration blocks, then you must add those features before compiling the programs with a C++ compiler. Some compiler products include a Standard C compiler in addition to the C++ compiler, and these restrictions do not exist if you use the C compiler.

C++ Keywords

When you port C programs to C++ you must be aware of the C++ keywords, which have meaning to the language and must not be used for identifiers. Older

C programs might well be using them. C++ reserves all of the Standard C key-words and adds those shown in the following list.

```
asm         private
catch       protected
class       public
delete      template
friend      this
inline      throw
new         try
operator    virtual
```

You will learn the meaning of all of these key words by the time you have fin-ished this book. There is one exception, however. The **asm** key word is imple-mentation dependent and is not addressed in this book.

Summary

This chapter gives you your first exposure to the C++ language. It identifies some of the language extensions and introduces C++ input/output streams so that you can use them in the exercises that follow. Chapter 2 discusses more of the improvements that C++ brings to the C language.

Chapter

2

C++ Extensions to C

Programmers often describe C++ as an improved C, because C++ offers better ways to write code within the structure of the C language. You already learned the first of those improvements in Chapter 1. Many programmers prefer the C++ double-slash (//) comment style to the /* and */ tokens of C.

This chapter introduces several other improvements that C++ brings to the language. These improvements enhance your use of C and prepare you for the more advanced object-oriented properties of C++. You will learn about:

- Default function arguments
- Variable declaration placement
- Scope resolution operator
- **inline** functions
- **const** variables and functions
- **enum** as a type
- Linkage-specifications
- Anonymous unions
- Unnamed function parameters
- Constructors for intrinsic types

19

Default Function Arguments

A C++ function prototype can declare that one or more of the function's parameters have default values. If you omit the corresponding arguments when you call the function, the compiler inserts the default values where it expects to see the argument.

You can declare default values for arguments in a C++ function prototype in the following:

```
void myfunc(int = 5, double = 1.23);
```

The expressions declare default values for the arguments. The C++ compiler substitutes the default values if you omit the arguments when you call the function. You can call the function by using any of the following:

```
myfunc(12, 3.45); // overrides both defaults
myfunc(3);        // effectively func(3, 1.23);
myfunc();         // effectively func(5, 1.23);
```

To omit the first parameter in these examples, you must omit the second one; however, you can omit the second parameter by itself. This rule applies to any number of parameters. You cannot omit a parameter unless you omit all of the parameters to its right.

Exercise 2.1 is an example of the use of default parameters.

```
#include <iostream.h>

void show(int = 1, float = 2.3, long = 4);

main()
{
    show();              // all three parameters default
    show(5);             // provide 1st parameter
    show(6, 7.8);        // provide 1st two
    show(9, 10.11, 12L); // provide all three parameters
}

void show(int first, float second, long third)
{
    cout << "\nfirst = "  << first;
    cout << ", second = " << second;
    cout << ", third = "  << third;
}
```

Exercise 2.1 A Program with Default Parameters in a Function Prototype.

Exercise 2.1, when you run it, displays the following result:

```
first = 1, second = 2.3, third = 4
first = 5, second = 2.3, third = 4
first = 6, second = 7.8, third = 4
first = 9, second = 10.11, third = 12
```

The first call to the **show** function in Exercise 2.1 allows the C++ compiler to provide the default values for the parameters just as the prototype specifies them. The second call provides the first parameter and allows the compiler to provide the other two. The third call provides the first two and allows the compiler to provide the last. The fourth call provides all three parameters, and none of the defaults are used.

Variable Declaration Placement

In C, you must declare all of the variables at the beginning of the block in which they have scope. You may not intermingle variable declaration and procedural expressions. C++ removes that restriction, allowing you to declare a variable anywhere before you reference it. This feature allows you to code the declaration of a variable closer to the code that uses it. When the declaration of a variable is near the code that uses it, the code becomes more readable. When you can see the variable's declaration in close proximity to its use, its purpose and behavior are easier to understand.

Exercise 2.2 places the declaration of a variable close to its first reference.

```
#include <iostream.h>

main()
{
    cout << "Enter a number: ";
    int n;
    cin >> n;
    cout << "The number is: " << n;
}
```

Exercise 2.2 Relocating a Variable Declaration.

Exercise 2.2 displays the following messages on the screen. The 234 is the number you enter.

```
Enter a number: 234
The number is: 234
```

The freedom to declare a variable anywhere in a block makes expressions such as the following one possible:

```
for(int ctr = 0; ctr < MAXCTR; ctr++)
    // ...
```

Exercise 2.3 declares a variable inside a **for** statement's expression list.

```
#include <iostream.h>

main()
{
    for (int lineno = 0; lineno < 5; lineno++)
        cout << "\nThis is line number: " << lineno;
}
```

Exercise 2.3 Variable Declaration Placement.

Exercise 2.3 produces the following output:

```
This is line number: 0
This is line number: 1
This is line number: 2
This is line number: 3
This is line number: 4
```

Note the scope of the **lineno** variable. The variable is in scope for the current block and all blocks subordinate to the current one. Its scope, however, begins where the declaration appears. C++ statements that appear before the declaration cannot refer to the variable even though they might appear in the same block as the variable's declaration.

The Scope Resolution Operator

In C, if a local variable and a global variable have the same name, all references to that name while the local variable is in scope refer to the local variable. Local variable names in C take precedence over global variable names. You must be aware of and program for this characteristic of C. If you want to refer to a global variable when a local one has the same name, you must change the name of one of the two.

C++ offers a different approach to this situation. You can tell the compiler that you want to refer to a global variable rather than the local one with the same name by using the :: scope resolution operator. The global scope resolution operator, which is coded as a prefix to the variable's name (for example, **::varname**), lets you explicitly reference a global variable from a scope where a local variable has the same name.

Exercise 2.4 is an example of how you use the scope resolution operator.

```
#include <iostream.h>

int amount = 123;        // a global variable

main()
{
    int amount = 456;    // a local variable

    cout << ::amount;    // display the global variable
    cout << ' ';
    cout << amount;      // display the local variable
}
```

Exercise 2.4 Global Scope Resolution Operator.

The exercise has two variables named **amount**. The first is global and contains the value 123. The second is local to the **main** function.

The first **cout** statement displays 123, the contents of the global **amount** variable because that reference to the variable name uses the :: global scope resolution operator. The second **cout** statement displays 456, the contents of the local **amount** variable because that reference to the variable name has no global scope resolution operator and defaults to the local variable in the traditional C fashion.

Exercise 2.4 displays the following output:

```
123 456
```

inline Functions

You can tell the C++ compiler that a function is **inline**, which compiles a new copy of the function each time it is called. The in-line nature of the individual copies eliminates the function calling overhead of a traditional function. You should use the inline function qualifier only when the function itself is small or when there are relatively few calls to the function.

Exercise 2.5 uses the **inline** keyword to make a small and frequently used function into an **inline** function.

```
#include <iostream.h>
#include <stdlib.h>

inline void error_message(char *s)
{
    cout << '\a' << '\n' << s;
    exit(1);
}

main()
{
    error_message("You called?");
}
```

Exercise 2.5 An in-line Function.

Exercise 2.5 sounds the computer's audible alarm and displays the message, "You called?" on the screen.

Observe that the exercise declares the **inline** function ahead of any calls to it. The *AT&T C++ Reference Manual* does not define under what conditions the compiler may choose to ignore the **inline** declaration except to say that the compiler may do so. Because of this ambiguity in the language specification, compiler builders have leeway in how they interpret the requirements. You could desire and declare an **inline** function (for performance reasons, perhaps) and have the compiler overrule you without saying so. Always declare **inline** functions ahead of all calls to them. If an **inline** function is to assume the appearance of an **extern** global function, that is, if it is to be called by code in several source files, put its declaration in a header file.

Inline functions are similar to **#define** macros with these exceptions: an **inline** function is subject to the same C++ type checking as normal functions; and **inline** functions are not subject to macro side effects. For example, consider this macro:

```
#define min(a,b) (a < b ? a : b)
```

The **min** macro has potential side effects. Suppose you called it this way:

```
int c = min(a++,b++);
```

The macro expansion, shown here, invokes undesirable side effects in that the lesser of the **a** and **b** variables is incremented twice.

```
int c = a++ < b++ ? a++ : b++;
```

The **inline** function calls, which the compiler treats like normal function calls, do not have such side effects.

The *const* Qualifier

The **const** qualifier adds the constant property to variables, pointers, and function parameters.

const Expressions

C++, like C, supports the **const** variable type qualifier. The **const** qualifier specifies that a variable is read-only. Nowhere other than through initialization can a program assign a value to a **const** identifier. C++ carries the **const** idea one step further and treats such identifiers as if they were true constant expressions. Wherever you can use a constant expression, you can use an identifier that has the **const** type qualifier.

Exercise 2.6 is an example of how you can use the **const** qualifier.

```
#include <iostream.h>

main()
{
    const int size = 5;
    char cs[size];

    cout << "The size of cs is " << sizeof cs;
}
```

*Exercise 2.6 The **const** Variable Qualifier.*

Exercise 2.6 displays the following message.

```
The size of cs is 5
```

const Pointers

You can qualify a pointer with **const** in one of two ways. The first usage specifies that the pointer may not be modified by the program, and it looks like this:

```
char *const cp = MyString;  // cannot modify cp
```

The **cp** pointer itself is constant. The program may not modify it. Therefore, the declaration must initialize the pointer to give it a value.

The second usage specifies that the program may not modify the object being pointed to by de-referencing the pointer. That usage looks like this:

```
const int *ip;  // cannot modify what ip points to
```

To combine the two usages and define a constant pointer to a constant object would look like this:

```
const int *const ip =;  // cannot modify either
```

const Function Parameters

The **prototype** and **declaration** block for a function can specify that a pointer parameter or what it points to is **const**. This usage looks like this:

```
void bar(const char *cp); // what cp points to is const
```

The **bar** function may not modify the character or character array that the **cp** pointer parameter points to.

It follows that you cannot pass a pointer to a **const** variable to a function that expects a pointer to a **non-const** variable. The function might assume that it can modify the object through the pointer. This situation is shown here:

```
void foobar(char *cp);    // cp -> non-const
const char *ccp = "123";
foobar(ccp);              // illegal: ccp -> const
```

const Return Values

A function can return a pointer to **const** as shown here:

```
const char *foo()
{
    return "foo";
}
```

The caller of **foo** cannot use the return pointer to modify what it points to. The caller cannot assign the return value to a pointer to a **non-const**. The caller cannot pass the return value to a function that is expecting a pointer to **non-const**. The caller cannot assign another value to the object that the return value points to. These restrictions are shown here:

```
const char *foo();       // foo returns pointer to const
char *cp = foo();        // illegal: cp -> non-const
strcpy(foo(), "bar");    // illegal: *foo() is const
const int *bar()         // bar returns pointer to const
*bar() = 123;            // illegal: *bar() is const
```

const Member Functions

Other uses of **const** are to qualify class and structure member functions to insure that they do not attempt to change any of the object's data members and to qualify references in function parameters. Chapters 6 and 7 discuss these usages.

enum as a Type

The **enum** in C++ is similar to **enum** in C, but with exceptions: All declarations of instances of a C **enum** must include the **enum** keyword. A C++ **enum** becomes a data type when you define it; therefore, once defined, it is known by its identifier alone, the same as any other type, and declarations may use the identifier name alone.

Exercise 2.7 demonstrates how a C++ program can reference an **enum** data type by using the identifier without the **enum** qualifier.

```
#include <iostream.h>

enum ignition_parts {
    distributor, cap, points, plug, condenser,
    coil, wires, done
};

main()
{
    ignition_parts ip;
    int p;
    do   {
        cout << "\nEnter part number (0-6, 7 to quit): ";
        cin >> p;
        ip = (ignition_parts) p;
        switch ( ip )   {
            case distributor: cout << "Distributor";
                                break;
            case cap:         cout << "Distributor cap";
                                break;
            case points:      cout << "Ignition points";
                                break;
            case plug:        cout << "Spark plug";
                                break;
            case condenser:   cout << "Condenser";
                                break;
            case coil:        cout << "Ignition coil";
                                break;
            case wires:       cout << "Coil, plug wires";
                                break;
```

*Exercise 2.7 **enum** as a Data Type.*

```
                case done:          break;
                default:            cout << "Unknown part number";
                                    break;
            }
        } while (ip != done);
    }
```

*Exercise 2.7 **enum** as a Data Type (continued).*

Exercise 2.7 displays these messages. You type the digits 0–6 and 7, followed by the **Enter** key after each of the prompts.

```
Enter part number (0-6, 7 to quit): 1
Distributor
Enter part number (0-6, 7 to quit): 2
Distributor cap
Enter part number (0-6, 7 to quit): 3
Ignition points
Enter part number (0-6, 7 to quit): 4
Spark plug
Enter part number (0-6, 7 to quit): 5
Condenser
Enter part number (0-6, 7 to quit): 6
Ignition coil
Enter part number (0-6, 7 to quit): 7
Coil, plug wires
Enter part number (0-6, 7 to quit): 0
```

This exercise translates a part number into its name. The **enum** associates the numbers 1–7 with identifiers that associate with the names of the parts. Observe that the declaration of the data item **ip** uses only the **enum** name, **ignition_parts**, and does not use the **enum** keyword itself. Because **ignition_parts** is a new data type, you do not need to further qualify it with the **enum** keyword.

Exercise 2.7 illustrates another difference between the C **enum** and the C++ **enum**. Observe that the program reads from **cin** into the **int** variable **p**. Then it casts **p** to an **ignition_parts** type and assigns it to **ip**. The **cin** object does not know how to read data into the new **ignition_parts** data type. In C, **enum**s and **int**s are interchangeable. Wherever you can use one, you can use the other. Not so in C++. Each **enum** is a distinct type subject to the strong type-checking of C++.

Linkage-Specifications

This next feature is not so much a C++ improvement to C as a way that the two languages can coexist. It is discussed here because later exercises use it.

A *linkage-specification* is the technique that C++ employs to make functions that were compiled by a different language compiler accessible to a C++ program. There may be differences in the way the two languages build external names. If you are calling functions that were compiled by a C compiler, you mut tell that fact to the C++ compiler.

The two languages may use different linkage systems to support type-safe linkage, a feature that insures that calls to functions in separately compiled source modules match the definitions of the functions with respect to parameter types. The C method is not as safe because it depends on every module using the same prototype, and you can override that assumption.

The C++ compiler internally modifies each function's name with suffixes that identify the parameter types. Use of these (so-called) mangled names allows duplicate function names to exist across separately compiled source files and allows the linker to properly resolve calls to the functions. The mangled names also transcend the use of prototypes to insure that the functions and their calls match. You cannot override the C++ type-checking simply by using different prototypes for the same function as you can in C.

A C compiler, for example, usually does not mangle function names. Therefore, you must tell the C++ compiler when a function has been (or must be) compiled with C linkage conventions.

Exercise 2.8 uses the linkage-specification to tell the C++ compiler that the functions in a header file are compiled by a C compiler.

```
#include <iostream.h>

extern "C"     {            // the linkage-specification
#include <stdlib.h>          // tells C++ that stdlib functions
}                            // were compiled with C


main()
{
    cout << rand();
}
```

Exercise 2.8 Linkage-Specifications.

Exercise 2.8 displays a value on the screen. The **extern "C"** statement says that everything within the brace-surrounded block—in this case, everything in the header file—is compiled by a C compiler. If you do not use the braces, the linkage-specification deals only with the declaration that immediately follows the C string.

Usually you put the linkage-specification in the header file that contains the prototypes for the C programs. Language environments that support both languages often manage the translation for you by hiding the linkage specification in the standard header files for the C functions. So, for the most part, you can be unaware of the difference between C functions and C++ functions. The exercises in this book assume that such files as *stdlib.h* and *string.h* include the appropriate linkage-specification.

There are times, however, when you need to use linkage-specifications outside the realm of standard C header files. If you have a large library of custom C functions to include in your C++ system, and you do not want to take the time and trouble to port them to C++ (perhaps you do not have the source code), then you must use a linkage-specification. If, within a C linkage-specification, you have some C++ prototypes, you can code a nested C++ linkage-specification.

Occasionally you need to tell the C++ compiler to compile a function with C linkage. You would do this if the function was to be called from a function that was itself compiled with C linkage (usually a function from your C library).

Exercise 2.9 is an example of a C++ program that calls a function that is compiled with a C compiler and has C linkage. The C++ program includes a function that is called from the C program and must be compiled with C linkage.

```
#include <iostream.h>

// --------- array of string pointers to be sorted
static const char *brothers[] = {
    "Frederick William",
    "Joseph Jensen",
    "Harry Alan",
    "Walter Ellsworth",
    "Julian Paul"
};

// ------ prototype of function compiled in C
extern "C" void SortCharArray(const char **);

// ------ C++ function to be called from the C program
extern "C"    {
  int SizeArray(void)
  {
      return sizeof brothers / sizeof (char*);
  }
}

main()
{
    // ---------- sort the pointers
    SortCharArray(brothers);
    // ---------- display the brothers in sorted order
    int size = SizeArray();
    for (int i = 0; i < size; i++)
        cout << '\n' << brothers[i];
}
```

Exercise 2.9a The C++ Source.

```
/* C program for linkage-specifications */
/*
 * A C program compiled with a C compiler to demonstrate
 * C linkage to a C++ program
 */

#include <string.h>
#include <stdlib.h>

static int comp(const void *a, const void *b);
int SizeArray(void); /* The C++ function */

void SortCharArray(const char **List)
{
    qsort(List, SizeArray(), sizeof(char *), comp);
}

/* ----- the compare function for qsort ---- */
static int comp(const void *a, const void *b)
{
    return strcmp(*(char **)a, *(char **)b);
}
```

Exercise 2.9b The C Source.

Exercise 2.9a displays these messages:

```
Frederick William
Harry Alan
Joseph Jensen
Julian Paul
Walter Ellsworth
```

Exercise 2.9 consists of two source files, a C++ program (2.9a) and a C function (2.9b). The C function sorts an array of character pointers but does not know the length of the array. It must, therefore, call a function—whose name must be **SizeArray** and which must be provided by the caller—to determine the length of the array. The C++ program declares two C linkages—one for the **SortCharArray** C function that the C++ program calls, and one for its own **SizeArray** function that the C function calls.

Without the linkage-specifications, the C++ compiler mangles the names of the C++ function and the C++ program's call to the C function. The linker is not able to resolve the C++ program's call to the **SortCharArray** C function or the C function's call to the **SizeArray** C++ function.

In the real world, you would take other measures to give the length of the array to the C function. You could null-terminate the array, and the C function could determine the array length on its own. You could pass the length of the array as an argument to the C function. You could pass the address of a function in the C++ program, which would then not need to be compiled with C linkage. Perhaps you are not in control of the C program, not having its source code, and you are stuck with whatever conventions the C programmer used. Perhaps the C function is already so widely used that you cannot change it.

Languages other than C and C++ can be supported by linkage-specifications, and their string values depend on the whims of the compiler builders.

Anonymous *Unions*

A C++ program can define an unnamed **union** anywhere it can have a variable. You might use this feature to save space, or you might use it to intentionally redefine a variable.

Exercise 2.10 illustrates the use of an anonymous **union**.

```
#include <iostream.h>

main()
{
    union    {
        int quantity_todate;
        int quantity_balance;
    };

    cout << "Enter quantity to date: ";
    cin >> quantity_todate;

    cout << "Enter quantity sold: ";
    int quantity_sold;
    cin >> quantity_sold;

    quantity_todate -= quantity_sold;
    cout << "Quantity balance = " << quantity_balance;
}
```

*Exercise 2.10 Anonymous **unions** .*

The program in Exercise 2.10 allows the two variables **quantity_todate** and **quantity_balance** to share the same space. After it subtracts **quantity_sold** from **quantity_todate**, **quantity_balance** contains the following result as well:

```
Enter quantity to date: 100
Enter quantity sold: 75
Quantity balance = 25
```

This feature eliminates a lot of **union** name prefixes in places where the only purpose for the **union** name is to support the **union**.

You must declare a global anonymous **union** as static.

Unnamed Function Parameters

You can declare a C function that has one or more parameters that the function does not use. This circumstance may occur when you write several functions that are called through a generic function pointer, for example. Some of the functions do not use all of the parameters. Following is an example of such a function.

```
int func(int x, int y)
{
    return x * 2;
}
```

Although this usage is correct, most C and C++ compilers complain that you failed to use the parameter named **y**. C++, however, allows you to declare functions with unnamed parameters to indicate to the compiler that the parameter exists, that the callers pass an argument for the parameter, but that the called function does not use it. Following is the C++ function coded with an unnamed second parameter.

```
int func(int x, int)
{
    return x * 2;
}
```

Constructors for Intrinsic Data Types

C++ allows you to initialize the intrinsic data types, such as **int**, **long**, **double**, etc., by using the notation of a class constructor. You will learn about class constructors in Chapter 7. The following statements are valid initialized variable declarations in C++.

```
int qty(123);
double spec(5.378);
```

The two statements just shown have the same effect as these traditional C declaration initialization statements.

```
int qty = 123;
double spec = 5.378;
```

Summary

You have learned ways that C++ improves the C language. Each subsequent chapter is more of the same, but the improvements that follow set C++ apart as its own language rather than just an improved C. You can use these new features in ways unrelated to the object-oriented paradigm, or you can totally immerse yourself in the paradigm and use C++ as your object-oriented development environment.

The C++ Free Store

This chapter is about the free store, the C++ mechanism that supports dynamic memory allocations. You will learn about:

- The **new** and **delete** operators
- Allocating dynamic arrays
- Dealing with out-of-memory conditions
- Installing custom **new** and **delete** operators

C programmers use the **malloc, calloc, realloc,** and **free** functions to allocate from and manage memory on the system heap. C++ offers a better way through the use of the **new** and **delete** operators of the C++ free store. These operators associate the allocation of memory with the way you use it. In the C++ lexicon, free store means heap, and **new** and **delete** are similar to **malloc** and **free**.

The *New* and *Delete* Operators

The **new** operator, when used with the name of a pointer to a data type, structure, or array, allocates memory for the item and assigns the address of that memory to the pointer.

The **delete** operator returns to the free store the memory owned by the object.

Exercise 3.1 is your first use of the **new** and **delete** operators.

```
#include <iostream.h>

struct Date {        // a date structure
    int month;
    int day;
    int year;
};

main()
{
    Date *birthday = new Date;  // get memory for a date
    birthday->month = 6;        // assign a value to the date
    birthday->day = 24;
    birthday->year = 1940;
    cout << "I was born on "    // display the date
        << birthday->month << '/'
```

*Exercise 3.1 The C++ Free Store: The **new** and **delete** Operators.*

```
            << birthday->day   << '/'
            << birthday->year;
     delete birthday;   // return memory to the free store
   }
```

*Exercise 3.1 The C++ Free Store: The **new** and **delete** Operators (continued).*

Exercise 3.1 displays this message:

```
   I was born on 6/24/1940
```

The structure in this exercise defines a date. The program uses the **new** operator to allocate memory for an instance of the structure. Then it assigns a date to the new structure. After displaying the contents of the structure, the program disposes of it by using the **delete** operator.

 The declaration of the **birthday** pointer does not include the **struct** keyword. This omission would appear to the C programmer to be an error. However, it is not an error but another of the improvements in C++. You will learn more about this in Chapter 5.

Allocating a Fixed-Dimension Array

The advantages of **new** and **delete** over the C functions **malloc** and **free** are not obvious in Exercise 3.1. They appear to be the same. However, **new** and **delete** provide a more readable syntax for memory allocation. Later, when you learn about classes and their constructors and destructors, you will encounter even more advantages of the **new** and **delete** operators.

Exercise 3.2 shows how you can use **new** and **delete** to acquire and then dispose of memory for an array.

```
#include <iostream.h>

main()
{
    int *birthday = new int[3];    // get memory for a date array
    birthday[0] = 6;               // assign a value to the date
    birthday[1] = 24;
    birthday[2] = 1940;
    cout << "I was born on "       // display the date
        << birthday[0] << '/'
        << birthday[1] << '/'
        << birthday[2];
    delete birthday;    // return memory to the free store
}
```

Exercise 3.2 The C++ Free Store: **new** *and* **delete** *with an Array.*

Exercise 3.2 displays the same message as Exercise 3.1.

Allocating Dynamic Arrays

Exercise 3.2 shows how the **new** operator accepts a data type with an array dimension. The dimension in the exercise is a constant 3, representing the number of integers in the date. You can, however, supply a variable dimension, and the **new** operator allocates the correct amount of memory.

Exercise 3.3 shows the use of a variably dimensioned array as allocated by the **new** operator.

```
#include <iostream.h>
#include <stdlib.h>

main()
{
    cout << "Enter the array size: ";
    int size;
    cin >> size;                    // get the array size
    int *array = new int[size];     // allocate an array
    for (int i = 0; i < size; i++)  // load the array
        array[i] = rand();          // with random numbers
    for (i = 0; i < size; i++)      // display the array
        cout << '\n' << array[i];
    delete array; // return the array to the free store
}
```

*Exercise 3.3 The C++ Free Store: **new** with a Dynamic Array.*

In running this exercise, you type in the size of the array. The **new** operator uses the value that you enter to establish the size of memory to be allocated. The program builds the array by using the **new** operator, fills it with random numbers, displays each of the elements in the array, and deletes the array by using the **delete** operator.

Exercise 3.3 displays the following messages: (The 5 is the number you would enter. The five other numbers are random numbers generated by the **rand**() function.)

```
Enter the array size: 5
346
130
10982
1090
11656
```

Exercise 3.4 offers another variation on the dynamically dimensioned array through the **new** operator. The exercise uses a function call to compute the dimension. The purpose is to read a number of variable-length strings from the user, sort them, and display them in a left-justified column.

```cpp
#include <iostream.h>
#include <stdlib.h>
#include <string.h>

// ---------- compare function to sort array of pointers
int comp(const void *a, const void *b)
{
    return strcmp(*(char **)a, *(char **)b);
}


main()
{
    cout << "How many names at most? ";
    int maxnames;
    cin >> maxnames;
    char **names = new char *[maxnames];
    char *name = new char[80];
    for (int namect = 0; namect < maxnames; namect++)     {
        cout << "Enter a name ('end' if done before "
                << maxnames << " names): ";
        cin >> name;
        if (strcmp(name, "end") == 0)
            break;
        names[namect] = new char[strlen(name)+1];
        strcpy(names[namect], name);
    }
```

Exercise 3.4 The C++ Free Store: More Dynamic Array Allocation.

```
    qsort(names, namect, sizeof(char *), comp);
    for (int i = 0; i < namect; i++)
        cout << names[i] << '\n';
    for (i = 0; i < namect; i++)
        delete names[i];
    delete name;
    delete names;
}
```

Exercise 3.4 The C++ Free Store: More Dynamic Array Allocation (continued).

Exercise 3.4 begins by asking you to enter the maximum number of names. From this value, the program allocates an array of character pointers. Then you begin entering names. For each name, the program allocates a new array with its address in the **names** array. When you enter the name "end" or after you have entered as many names as you said you would, the program displays all of them.

Exercise 3.4 displays these messages: (The 6 is the number of names you intend to enter. The Bill, Sam, Paul, Spoof, Jim, and Chick entries are the names you could enter. The sorted list of the same names follows the entries.)

```
How many names at most? 6
Enter a name ('end' if done before 6 names): Bill
Enter a name ('end' if done before 6 names): Sam
Enter a name ('end' if done before 6 names): Paul
Enter a name ('end' if done before 6 names): Spoof
Enter a name ('end' if done before 6 names): Jim
Enter a name ('end' if done before 6 names): Chick
Bill
Chick
Jim
Paul
Sam
Spoof
```

The program in Exercise 3.4 does not compile with Zortech C++. That compiler requires the **extern "C"** linkage specification around the definition of the **comp** function even though you are passing the address of a C++ function and not asking the C function to call a specifically named C++ function. Other C++ implementations do not require the linkage specification in this context.

When the Store is Exhausted

These exercises have not considered the question of what to do if the free store is out of memory when you use the **new** operator. Instead, they just assume that the store is never exhausted. Clearly, this is not a real-world approach. The C **malloc** function returns a null pointer under that condition, and C programs that call **malloc** usually test for the null return and do something meaningful about it.

The _new_handler Function Pointer

You could take the same approach with C++ by simply testing each use of the **new** operator for a null return; **new** returns a null pointer if there is no memory to allocate. There is a better way, however. C++ includes an internal function pointer named **_new_handler**. Normally, that pointer is null, and when **new** runs out of memory, **new** returns null. But if the **_new_handler** function pointer contains a non-null value, **new** assumes that the value is the address to call when memory is exhausted.

The set_new_handler Function

C++ includes a function named **set_new_handler** that lets you set the **_new_handler** function pointer.

Exhausting the Free Store

If the new operator finds itself out of free-store space, it calls the function pointed to by **_new_handler**. Exercise 3.5 illustrates a **_new_handler** function that terminates the program when the free store is gone.

```
#include <iostream.h>
#include <stdlib.h>
#include <new.h>

static void all_gone()
{
    cerr << "\n\aThe free store is empty\n";
    exit(1);
}

main()
{
    set_new_handler(all_gone);
    long total = 0;
    while (1)    {
        char *gobble = new char[10000];
        total += 10000;
        cout << "Got 10000 for a total of " << total << '\n';
    }
}
```

*Exercise 3.5 Free Store Exhaustion and the **_new_handler** Function.*

This exercise goes into a loop consuming free store and displaying messages about it. When the store is empty, the **new** operator turns things over to the **all_gone** function, which sends an error message to **cerr** and exits.

Exercise 3.5 would display the following messages:

```
Got 10000 for a total of 10000
Got 10000 for a total of 20000
Got 10000 for a total of 30000
Got 10000 for a total of 40000
```

```
Got 10000 for a total of 50000
Got 10000 for a total of 60000
The free store is empty
```

 The Microsoft C++ 7.0 compiler implements **set_new_handler** in an unconventional manner, and Exercise 3.5 does not work with that compiler. Refer to the Microsoft documentation for a description of its implementation of **set_new_handler**.

Going for More Store

If your **_new_handler** function returns, the **new** operator tries again to allocate the required memory. This opens the door for a programmer to try to do something about free-store exhaustion. What you do would depend on how your free store works. The default **new** and **delete** operators take their memory from the heap. Heap management is an implementation-dependent operation, and anything you might do to increase the memory available to the default **new** operator would not be portable to other systems, perhaps not even to other C++ compilers on the same system.

Rolling Your Own *new* and *delete* Operators

The default **new** and **delete** operators are general purpose enough to suffice for most programming situations. There could be times, however, when your program wants more control over what happens when the **new** operator executes. For example, the default **new** operator does not initialize the memory that is allocated. Perhaps you want to set all of the space to zeros. To do this, you build your own **new** operator.

You are about to learn how to install your own dynamic memory manager into your C++ environment. This ability implies a certain amount of responsibility. Overloading the global **new** and **delete** operators puts your functions in the position of allocating and freeing dynamic memory for all global uses of the free store, including **new** and **delete** calls from within the compiler's library functions and startup code. Although C++ provides this powerful overloading facility, most programmers do not find it necessary to replace the global **new** and **delete** functions provided by the compiler.

Exercise 3.6 is an example of a custom-built **new** operator that initializes memory to zeros before returning.

```
#include <iostream.h>
#include <stdlib.h>

// ------------ overloaded new operator
void *operator new(size_t size)
{
    void *rtn = calloc(1, size);
    return rtn;
}

// ---------- overloaded delete operator
void operator delete(void *type)
{
    free(type);
}

main()
{
    // ------ allocate a zero-filled array
    int *ip = new int[10];
    // ------ display the array
    for (int i = 0; i < 10; i++)
        cout << ' ' << ip[i];
    // ----- release the memory
    delete ip;
}
```

*Exercise 3.6 Home-brew **new** and **delete**.*

Exercise 3.6 displays this message of zero values:

```
0 0 0 0 0 0 0 0 0 0
```

This exercise is an early look at operator overloading, a powerful feature of C++. The **new** and **delete** keywords are implemented in C++ as operators, and you can redefine their meaning within the context of how they are called by writing **operator** functions that replace them. Chapter 8 is dedicated to the subject of overloaded operators for the C++ classes that you develop.

The overloaded **new** operator in Exercise 3-6 uses the standard C **calloc** function to get memory. That function allocates memory and sets it to zero, so your work is done for you.

Exercise 3.7 shows how you can build and use an overloaded **new** operator with additional parameters. For this exercise, the **new** operator fills memory with a character selected by your use of the operator.

```cpp
#include <iostream.h>
#include <stdlib.h>
#include <string.h>

// ------------- overloaded new operator
void *operator new(size_t size, int filler)
{
    void *rtn;
    if ((rtn = malloc(size)) != 0)
        memset(rtn, filler, size);
    return rtn;
}
```

*Exercise 3.7 Home-Brew **new** and **delete** with Character Fill.*

```
// ---------- overloaded delete operator
void operator delete(void *type)
{
    free(type);
}


main()
{
    // ------ allocate an asterisk-filled array
    char *cp = new ('*') char[10];
    // ------ display the array
    for (int i = 0; i < 10; i++)
        cout << ' ' << cp[i];
    // ----- release the memory
    delete cp;
}
```

*Exercise 3.7 Home-Brew **new** and **delete** with Character Fill.*

This exercise shows you how to add parameters to the **new** operator. The first parameter must be of type **size_t** and, in the default **new**, is the *only* parameter. But you can provide additional parameters as shown in Exercise 3.7. The use of the **new** operator in that exercise shows you how to pass parameters to the overloaded **new**.

None of these overloaded **new** operators acknowledges the role of the **_new_handler** function pointer. It is with an overloaded **new** operator that you can take advantage of this feature. Because you supply the memory allocator, you are in the best position to develop the strategy for dealing with memory exhaustion.

Exercise 3.8 shows how to connect your **new** operator to your custom **_new_handler** function, without actually solving the problem of memory exhaustion.

```
#include <iostream.h>
#include <stdlib.h>
#include <string.h>
#include <new.h>

static void all_gone()
{
    cerr << "\n\aThe free store is empty\n";
    exit(1);
}

// ------------- overloaded new operator
void *operator new(size_t size)
{
    void *rtn;
    if ((rtn = malloc(size)) == 0)
        all_gone();
    return rtn;
}

// ----------- overloaded delete operator
void operator delete(void *type)
{
    free(type);
}
```

*Exercise 3.8 Home-Brew **new** and **delete** with a custom **_new_handler**.*

```
main()
{
    set_new_handler(all_gone);
    char *ip;
    // ----- get more heap than exists
    for (;;)
        ip = new char[30000];
}
```

*Exercise 3.8 Home-Brew **new** and **delete** with a custom __new_handler__ (continued).*

Exercise 3.8 sounds the audible alarm and displays this message:

```
The free store is empty
```

The Microsoft C++ 7.0 compiler implements **set_new_handler** in an unconventional manner, and as with Exercise 3.5, Exercise 3.8 does not work with that compiler. Refer to the Microsoft documentation for a description of its implementation of **set_new_handler**.

You can use your custom **new** operator and the default **new** operator in the same program if the custom **new** has different parameter types than the default one.

Exercise 3.9 illustrates how the compiler selects the correct **new** operator function to call based on the types of the parameters in the use of the **new** operator.

```
#include <iostream.h>
#include <stdlib.h>
#include <string.h>

// ------------- overloaded new operator
void *operator new(size_t size, int filler)
{
    cout << "\nRunning new\n";
    void *rtn = malloc(size);
    if (rtn != 0)
        memset(rtn, filler, size);
    return rtn;
}


// ----------- overloaded delete operator
void operator delete(void *type)
{
    cout << "\nDeleting";
    free(type);
}


main()
{
    // ------ allocate an array with the custom new
    char *cp = new ('*') char[10];
    // ---- use the default new for this allocation
    int *ip = new int[10];
    // ----- release the memory (both use our delete)
    delete ip;
    delete cp;
}
```

*Exercise 3.9 Home-Brew **new** and **delete** with Delete Contention.*

There is an anomaly to this usage, however. Because you can overload the **delete** operator only with its originally defined **void*** parameter, your custom **delete** function executes for all of your uses of **delete**. This is not true when you build custom **new** and **delete** operators for C++ classes. (You are not at that point yet; wait until Chapter 7.)

Exercise 3.9 displays messages on the console each time the **new** and **delete** operators execute. The following output is what the exercise displays:

```
Running new
Deleting
Deleting
```

As you can see, the custom **new** executes once, but the custom **delete** executes twice. The only way you can be sure that this works is to know that in your C++ environment, the default **delete** calls the C **free** function, and that might not always be the case. As a rule, you should overload the **new** and **delete** operators only in the context where you use the overloaded versions exclusively.

NOTE Exercises 3.6 through 3.9 overload the global **new** and **delete** operators. The Microsoft C++ compiler and CFRONT ports that use the Microsoft compiler (Comeau C++, for example) do not link correctly because the Microsoft linker finds a collision between the default global functions that implement these operators and the overloaded ones. To get the link to work, you must use the linker's /NOE command line parameter. The batch files on the companion diskette show you how to do this.

Summary

This chapter dealt with the basics of the C++ free store and the **new** and **delete** operators. You will learn more about these aspects of C++ in later chapters where their advanced features contribute to C++ class construction.

During your excursion into **new** and **delete**, you received an introduction to overloaded operators. Overloading is one of the more powerful facilities in C++. You can overload operators, and you can overload functions. Chapter 4 deals with the overloading of functions.

Chapter

4

Overloaded Functions

This chapter is about *function overloading*, the C++ technique that allows you to give more than one function the same name. You will learn about:

- Overloading to change functionality
- Overloading to accomodate different data formats

You can reuse a function name in a C program if you want the **new** function and the old one is not in scope. The two functions cannot, however, share the same scope. If you want to have two similar C functions with slightly different operations on different parameter types, you must write two different C functions. The standard C **strcpy** and **strncpy** functions are examples.

C++ has a better way. It allows you to reuse a function name in the same scope, but with different parameter types. Both versions of the function are then available at the same time. This feature, called function overloading, is when you define multiple versions of the same function name.

Overloading for Different Operations

Sometimes you overload a function because it performs a generic task, but there are different permutations of what it does. The standard C **strcpy** and **strncpy** functions are examples. Both functions copy strings, but they do so in slightly different ways. The **strcpy** function simply copies a string from the source to the destination. The **strncpy** function copies a string, but stops copying when the source string terminates or after it copies a specified number of characters. These functions are likely candidates to be members of an overloaded function family.

Exercise 4.1 replaces the standard C **strcpy** and **strncpy** functions with the single function name, **string_copy**.

```
#include <iostream.h>

void string_copy(char *dest, const char *src)
{
    while((*dest++ = *src++) != '\0')

        ;
}
```

Exercise 4.1 Overloading Functions for Different Operations.

```
void string_copy(char *dest, const char *src, int len)
{
    while (len && (*dest++ = *src++) != '\0')
        --len;
    while (len--)
        *dest++ = '\0';
}


static char misspiggie[20], kermit[20];


main()
{
    string_copy(misspiggie, "Miss Piggie");
    string_copy(kermit,
        "Kermit the file transfer protocol", 6);
    cout << kermit << " and " << misspiggie;
}
```

Exercise 4.1 Overloading Functions for Different Operations (continued).

Exercise 4.1 displays this message:

```
Kermit and Miss Piggie
```

There are two functions named **string_copy** in this program. What sets them apart is their different parameter lists. The first of the two **string_copy** functions has destination and source character pointers as parameters. The second function has the pointers and an integer length as well. The C++ compiler recognizes that these are two distinct functions by virtue of these differences in their parameter lists.

Overloading for Different Formats

Exercise 4.1 showed how you might overload a function to get a different algorithm on similar data. Another reason to overload a function is to get the same result from data values that can be represented in different formats. Standard C has different ways of representing the date and time. You will find more ways in Unix and still others in MS-DOS.

Exercise 4.2 shows how you can send two of the standard C formats to the overloaded **display_time** functions.

```cpp
#include <iostream.h>
#include <time.h>

void display_time(const struct tm *tim)
{
    cout << "1. It is now " << asctime(tim);
}

void display_time(time_t *tim)
{
    cout << "2. It is now " << ctime(tim);
}

main()
{
    time_t tim = time(0);
    struct tm *ltim = localtime(&tim);

    display_time(ltim);
    display_time(&tim);
}
```

Exercise 4.2 Overloaded Functions for Different Data Formats.

Exercise 4.2 uses the standard C data formats **time_t** and **struct tm**. It gets the value of the current date and time into them with the **time** and **localtime** functions. Then it calls its own overloaded **display_time** function for each of the formats.

Exercise 4.2 displays the following results:

```
1. It is now Wed May 12 12:05:20 1993
2. It is now Wed May 12 12:05:20 1993
```

Dates and times are good ways to experiment with overloaded functions. There are many ways to internally represent them, many ways that different systems report them to a program, and many ways to display them. In addition to all of these formats, there are many common date and time algorithms. A comprehensive date and time package would be a solid addition to any programmer's tool collection.

Summary

Function overloading is one of the facets of C++ that supports the object-oriented programming view of things. However, as this chapter shows, you can use its features in your traditional programming environment to design and develop programs that are more readable.

C++ Structures

This chapter describes how C++ enhances the programmer's use of structures. You will learn about:

- Structures as data types
- Structures with function members
- Access specifiers
- C++ unions

C++ structures are similar to C structures but they have more features. This chapter describes the characteristics of the C++ structure that distinguishes it from C in a way that brings the programmer closer to the object-oriented paradigm.

Structures as Data Types

When you define a structure in C++, you have designed a new data type and added it to the language. In C, however, every declaration of an instance of a defined **structure** must include the struct keyword, as in the following example:

```
/* --- defining a C structure --- */
struct Date {int month,day,year;};
/* --- declaring a C structure --- */
struct Date today;
```

In C++, a structure is its own data type and can be known by its own name without the **struct** keyword.

Exercise 5.1 shows the various ways you can use a structure's name in C++.

```
#include <iostream.h>

// ------  structure - data type
struct Date {
    int month;
    int day;
    int year;
};
static void display(Date);          // a date parameter
```

Exercise 5.1 The Structure as a Data Type.

```
main()
{
    static Date birthday = {10,12,1962}; // a date
    Date dates[10];                      // an array of dates
    Date *dp = dates;                    // a pointer to a date

    for (int i = 0; i < 10; i++)    {
        *(dp + i) = birthday;
        dates[i].year += i;
        cout << "\nOn ";
        display(dates[i]);
        cout << " Sharon was ";
        if (i > 0)
            cout << i;
        else
            cout << "born";
    }
}

static void display(Date dt)
{
    static char *mon[] = {
        "January","February","March","April","May","June",
        "July","August","September","October","November",
        "December"};
    cout << mon[dt.month-1] << ' ' << dt.day << ", "
        << dt.year;
}
```

Exercise 5.1 The Structure as a Data Type (continued).

Exercise 5.1 defines a **Date** structure with a member for each of the elements **day**, **month**, and **year**. The **main** function contains an instance of the structure, an array of the structure, and a pointer to the structure. The program includes a prototype of a function that accepts the structure as a parameter. Yet the keyword **struct** does not appear in any of these objects because **Date** became a data type when the structure was defined.

Exercise 5.1 displays the following messages:

```
On October 12, 1962 Sharon was born
On October 12, 1963 Sharon was 1
On October 12, 1964 Sharon was 2
On October 12, 1965 Sharon was 3
On October 12, 1966 Sharon was 4
On October 12, 1967 Sharon was 5
On October 12, 1968 Sharon was 6
On October 12, 1969 Sharon was 7
On October 12, 1970 Sharon was 8
On October 12, 1971 Sharon was 9
```

Structures with Functions

A structure is an aggregate of data types. Grouping the different members forms a record of sorts with different fields. The structure can contain integers, floats, arrays, pointers, typedefs, unions, and other data types. In other words, any valid data type can be a member of a structure. This convention is consistent with the C definition of a structure. C++ adds another type of member to the structure. In C++, structures can include functions.

A Glimpse at Object-Oriented Programming

Take a moment to consider the implications of what you just learned. By adding functions to structures, you add the ability for a structure to include algorithms that are bound to, and work with, the other structure members. You closely associate the algorithms with the data they process; this is called *encapsulation*, and it is one of the fundamental concepts of the object-oriented program.

Adding Functions to Structures

Exercise 5.2 is a program that adds a function to the **Date** structure in Exercise 5.1. The function's name is **display**, and its purpose is to display the contents of an instance of the **Date** structure.

```
#include <iostream.h>

// ------ structure with a function
struct Date {
    int month, day, year;
    void display();    // a function to display the date
};

void Date::display()
{
    static char *mon[] = {
        "January","February","March","April","May","June",
        "July","August","September","October","November",
        "December"};
    cout << mon[month-1] << ' ' << day << ", " << year;
}

main()
{
    static Date birthday = {4, 6, 1961};
    cout << "Alan's date of birth was ";
    birthday.display();
}
```

Exercise 5.2 Structures with Functions.

Exercise 5.2 codes the **display** function's declaration as **Date::display**. This notation tells the C++ compiler that the **display** function exists to support instances of the **Date** structure. In fact, the only way to call this **display** function is as a member of a declared **Date**.

The **main** function declares a **Date** named **birthday** and initializes it with a value. Then the **main** function calls the **Date::display** function by identifying it as a member of the **birthday** structure using the following notation:

```
birthday.display();
```

The **Date::display** function displays the following date format:

```
Alan's date of birth was April 6, 1961
```

The **Date::display** function can reference members of the structure with which it is associated directly without naming an instance of the structure, because it is a member of the structure.

Multiple Instances of the Same Structure

As you might expect, you can declare more than one instance of the same structure, and the member function associates itself with the data in the particular structure for which you call it.

Exercise 5.3 uses the **Date** structure in two places.

```
#include <iostream.h>

// ------ structure with a function
struct Date {
    int month, day, year;
    void display();   // a function to display the date
};
```

Exercise 5.3 Multiple Instances of a Structure with a Function.

```
void Date::display()
{
    static char *mon[] = {
        "January","February","March","April","May","June",
        "July","August","September","October","November",
        "December"};
    cout << mon[month-1] << ' ' << day << ", " << year;
}


main()
{
    static Date alans_birthday = {4, 6, 1961};
    cout << "\nAlan's date of birth was ";
    alans_birthday.display();

    static Date wendys_birthday = {4, 28, 1965};
    cout << "\nWendy's date of birth was ";
    wendys_birthday.display();
}
```

Exercise 5.3 Multiple Instances of a Structure with a Function (continued).

The program declares two **Date** structures and uses the **display** function to display the following messages:

```
Alan's date of birth was April 6, 1961
Wendy's date of birth was April 28, 1965
```

Overloaded Structure Functions

You can have different structure definitions that use the same function name. This is another form of function overloading you learned about in Chapter 4.

Exercise 5.4 is an example of two structures that each use a function named **display**.

```cpp
#include <iostream.h>
#include <stdio.h>
#include <time.h>

// ------  date structure with a function
struct Date {
    int month, day, year;
    void display();        // a function to display the date
};

void Date::display()
{
    static char *mon[] = {
        "January","February","March","April","May","June",
        "July","August","September","October","November",
        "December"};
    cout << mon[month] << ' ' << day << ", " << year;
}

// ------  time structure with a function
struct Time {
    int hour, minute, second;
    void display(void);   // a function to display the clock
};

void Time::display()
{
```

Exercise 5.4 Two Structures with the Same Function Name.

```
        char tmsg[15];
        sprintf(tmsg, "%d:%02d:%02d %s",
            (hour > 12 ? hour - 12 : (hour == 0 ? 12 : hour)),
            minute, second,
            hour < 12 ? "am" : "pm");
        cout << tmsg;
    }

main()
{
    // -------- get the current time from the OS
    time_t curtime = time(0);
    struct tm tim = *localtime(&curtime);
    // --------- clock and date structures
    Time now;
    Date today;
    // --------- initialize the structures
    now.hour = tim.tm_hour;
    now.minute = tim.tm_min;
    now.second = tim.tm_sec;
    today.month = tim.tm_mon;
    today.day = tim.tm_mday;
    today.year = tim.tm_year+1900;
    // ---------- display the date and time
    cout << "At the tone it will be ";
    now.display();
    cout << " on ";
    today.display();
    cout << '\a';
    }
```

Exercise 5.4 Two Structures with the Same Function Name (continued).

The program in Exercise 5.4 has a **Date** structure and a **Time** structure. Both structures have functions named **display**. The **display** function that is associated with the Date structure displays the date; the **display** function that is associated with the **Time** function displays the time.

Exercise 5.4 sounds the audible alarm and displays the following message.

```
At the tone it will be 6:19:12 pm on May 3, 1991
```

The date and time in the display will be the current ones when you run the program.

Access Specifiers

By default, the members of a structure are visible to all the functions that are within the scope of the structure object. You can limit this outside access with three "access specifiers" in the structure's definition. The **Date** structure in the earlier exercises might be modified with the **private** and **public** access specifiers as shown here.

```
struct Date {
private:
    int month, day, year;
public:
    void display(void);
};
```

All members following the **private** access specifier are accessible only to the member functions within the structure definition. All members following the **public** access specifier are accessible to any function that is within the scope of the structure. If you omit the access specifiers, everything is public. You can use an access specifier more than once in the same structure definition.

The **protected** access specifier is the same as the **private** access specifier unless the structure is a part of a class hierarchy, a subject that Chapter 9 addresses.

When you define a structure with the **private** and **protected** access specifiers, the structure begins to take on the properties of a class, and you should define it as such. You cannot, for example, initialize the structure shown above with a brace-separated list of integers because the data members are private to the class's member functions and are not visible to the rest of the program. You would need to define a "constructor" function, and perhaps a "destructor" function, to handle the structure's initialization when it comes into scope and destruction when it goes out of scope. These subjects take on meaning when you learn about C++ classes in Chapter 7.

Unions

C++ **unions** are similar to C **unions** in that the data members share the same memory, and only one of the members can contain a value at any one time. (You learned about C++ anonymous **unions** in Chapter 2.) C++ **unions** share some of the enhancements that C++ structures have. A **union** can have function members but it cannot be a part of a class hierarchy the way structures can. You will learn about classes in Chapter 7 and class hierarchies in Chapter 9. A **union** can have constructor and destructor functions (Chapter 7), but it cannot have any virtual functions (Chapter 9).

Unions can have private, protected, and public members. You will learn more about access specifiers in Chapter 7.

Summary

This chapter has moved you closer to object-oriented programming. Structures that become data types and have functions associated with them resemble closely the C++ class, which is the basic unit of the object-oriented paradigm. Chapter 6 discusses the C++ reference, a way to avoid the sometimes confusing world of the C pointer.

References

This chapter is about the C++ reference. You will learn about:

- What you can and cannot do with a reference
- The alias nature of a reference variable
- How and when to initialize a reference
- Passing references to functions
- Returning references from functions

The *reference* variable is an alias or synonym for another variable. It is used most often for passing parameters and returning values by reference rather than by value. The reference lets you pass and return large data structures without the overhead of copying them.

The reference is also a way to avoid pointer de-referencing syntax in your code.

If you are like most C programmers, the pointer gave you the most trouble when you first learned C. Veteran C programmers can still get bogged down trying to comprehend some of the complex operations that C pointers and pointers-to-pointers permit. The C++ reference variable can give you some of the same kind of trouble until you understand it, and it has some of its own wrinkles as well. Its syntax and usage, however, prevent many of the pointer pitfalls that trap C programmers.

Following is a list of things to remember when you deal with references. You will learn about each of these items in the paragraphs and exercises ahead in this chapter.

- A reference is an alias for an object.
- A reference must be initialized and cannot be changed.
- References work well with user-defined data types.
- You can pass references to functions.
- You can return references from functions.
- A function that returns a reference can appear on either side of an assignment.
- You cannot do these things with references:
  - point to them
  - have an array of them
  - take the address of one
  - compare them
  - assign to them
  - do arithmetic to them
  - modify them

The Reference Is an Alias

A C++ reference is an alias for an object. When you declare a reference, you give it a value that you may not change for the life of the reference. The **&** operator identifies a reference variable as in the following example:

```
int actualint;
int& otherint = actualint;
```

These statements declare an integer, named **actualint**, which has another name, **otherint**. Now all references to either name have the same effect.

Exercise 6.1 illustrates how a reference and the data item it refers to appear to be one and the same.

```
#include <iostream.h>

main()
{
    int actualint = 123;
    int& otherint = actualint;

    cout << '\n' << actualint;
    cout << '\n' << otherint;
    otherint++;
    cout << '\n' << actualint;
    cout << '\n' << otherint;
    actualint++;
    cout << '\n' << actualint;
    cout << '\n' << otherint;
}
```

Exercise 6.1 The Reference.

This exercise shows that operations on **otherint** act upon actualint. Exercise 6.1 displays the following output, and it shows that whatever you do to **otherint**, you do to **actualint**, and vice versa:

```
123
123
124
124
125
125
```

The alias metaphor is almost a perfect one. A reference is neither a copy of nor a pointer to the thing to which it refers. Instead, it is another name that the compiler recognizes for the thing to which it refers.

Exercise 6.2 demonstrates the alias metaphor by displaying the addresses of both identifiers. When you run the exercise, you see that they both have the same address.

```
#include <iostream.h>

main()
{
    int actualint = 123;
    int& otherint = actualint;

    cout << &actualint << ' ' << &otherint;
}
```

Exercise 6.2 Addresses of References.

Exercise 6.2 displays the following message.

```
0x3b96fff4 0x3b96fff4
```

The format and values of these addresses depend on where your run-time system locates the variables, and the format of the hexadecimal address in your compiler. The point here is not what the addresses are, but that they are the same.

Although the reference variable is described as an alias, it is a data item unto itself and not the same kind of alias that you get by using the preprocessor's **#define** statement. While a reference apparently delivers the behavior of a **#defined** alias, it is in fact separate. It is variable because, at different times in the execution of a program, some references can be initialized to refer to different objects.

Initializing a Reference

A reference is of no use until it refers to something. Unlike a pointer, a reference is not a variable that you can manipulate. It is, as you learned in the first two exercises in this chapter, an alias for something real. Therefore, it is only natural that you must initialize a reference (explicitly give the reference something to refer to) when you define it, unless:

1. It is declared with **extern**, in which case it would have been initialized elsewhere.

2. It is a member of a class, in which case the constructor function of the class initializes it.

3. It is being declared as a parameter in a function declaration, in which case its value is established by the caller's argument when the function is called.

4. It is declared as the return type of a function, in which case its value is established when the function returns something.

As you work through the exercises in this and later chapters, observe all uses of references to see that each one matches one of these criteria.

References to User-Defined Data Types

Most programmers use references primarily to refer to structure and class objects and avoid references to the standard C++ data types. References are not as useful when they refer to **ints**, **longs**, and the like. An advantage of references is that they reduce the overhead involved with passing and returning parameters to and from functions. This advantage does not exist for references to the smaller data types, because passing the original data type is as efficient as passing a reference.

References as Function Parameters

References are often used as function parameters. There is little need to build a reference that exists only in the view of the variable that it refers to. You might just as well use the original name of the variable. The exercises in this chapter up until now have used references in that way, but the purpose of those exercises was to show you the behavior of references, not necessarily the best way to use them.

References as function parameters offer three advantages:

1.   They eliminate the overhead associated with passing large data structures as parameters.

2.   They eliminate the pointer de-referencing notation used in functions to which you pass references to parameters.

3.   They allow the called function to operate on and possibly modify the caller's copy of the data.

These advantages are illustrated in the next set of exercises.

Reference Parameters to Eliminate Copies

By using a reference as a function parameter, you avoid the overhead of passing large structures to functions, much the same way you do when you pass pointers to functions.

Exercise 6.3 illustrates the difference between passing a structure and passing a reference to a structure.

```
#include <iostream.h>

// ---------- a big structure
struct bigone    {
    int serno;
    char text[1000];    // a lot of chars
} bo = { 123, "This is a BIG structure"};

// -- two functions that have the structure as a parameter
void slowfunc(bigone p1);        // call by value
void fastfunc(bigone& p1);       // call by reference

main()
{
    slowfunc(bo);    // this will take a while
    fastfunc(bo);    // this will be a snap
}

// ---- a call-by-value function
void slowfunc(bigone p1)
{
    cout << '\n' << p1.serno;
    cout << '\n' << p1.text;
}

// ---- a call by reference function
void fastfunc(bigone& p1)
{
    cout << '\n' << p1.serno;
    cout << '\n' << p1.text;
}
```

Exercise 6.3 Reference Parameters Reduce Overhead.

Exercise 6.3 displays these messages.

```
123
This is a BIG structure
123
This is a BIG structure
```

Unfortunately, nothing in the exercise jumps out at you to prove the point. The only apparent difference is the use of the **&** reference operator in the function's prototype and parameter declaration. But the differences are real.

Suppose the character array in the **bigone** structure was 20,000 bytes instead of 1,000. The program could fail on the first function call because C++ passes parameters on the stack, and the stack might not be big enough. You would need to use a Compiler option to specify a bigger stack just to support this one function call. By passing a reference to the function, you don't have to worry about it.

References to Eliminate Pointer De-Referencing

By using a reference in the called function instead of a pointer, you avoid the pointer de-referencing operators that can make pointer usage difficult to read.

Exercise 6.4 illustrates the difference between reference notation and pointer notation.

```
#include <iostream.h>

// ---------- a big structure
struct bigone    {
    int serno;
    char text[1000];    // a lot of chars
} bo = { 123, "This is a BIG structure"};
```

Exercise 6.4 Reference Parameters Eliminate Pointer Notation.

```
// -- two functions that have the structure as a parameter
void ptrfunc(bigone *p1);        // call by pointer
void reffunc(bigone& p1);        // call by reference

main()
{
    ptrfunc(&bo);    // pass the address
    reffunc(bo);     // pass the reference
}

// ---- a pointer function
void ptrfunc(bigone *p1)
{
    cout << '\n' << p1->serno;        // pointer notation
    cout << '\n' << p1->text;
}

// ---- a call by reference function
void reffunc(bigone& p1)
{
    cout << '\n' << p1.serno;         // reference notation
    cout << '\n' << p1.text;
}
```

Exercise 6.4 Reference Parameters Eliminate Pointer Notation (continued).

Exercise 6.4 displays the same messages as Exercise 6.3.

You might argue that there is little about the pointer notation in Exercise 6.4 to make it less readable than that of the reference notation. This perceived advantage is one of personal choice. The differences are more dramatic in a function with a lot of pointer de-referencing.

Call-By-Reference

When one function passes a reference to another function, the called function is working on the caller's copy of the parameter, not a local copy (as it does when you pass the variable itself). This behavior is known as *call-by-reference*. The more conventional C parameter behavior of passing the parameter's value to a private copy in the called function is known as *call-by-value*.

If the called function changes a reference parameter, it is changing the caller's copy.

Exercise 6.5 shows how reference parameters allow a **swapper** function to swap the parameters of the caller.

```
#include <iostream.h>

// ------ simple date class
struct Date {
    int da, mo, yr;
    void display();
};
void Date::display()
{
    cout << da << '/' << mo << '/' << yr;
}
void swapper(Date&, Date&);
void display(Date&, Date&);

main()
{
    static Date now = {23,2,90};    // two dates
    static Date then = {10,9,60};
```

Exercise 6.5 Call-By-Reference.

```
        display(now, then);         // display the dates
        swapper(now, then);         // swap them
        display(now, then);         // display them swapped
    }

    // ----- this function swaps the caller's dates
    void swapper(Date& dt1, Date& dt2)
    {
        Date save;
        save = dt1;
        dt1 = dt2;
        dt2 = save;
    }

    void display(Date& now, Date& then)
    {
        cout << "\n Now:  ";
        now.display();
        cout << "\n Then: ";
        then.display();
    }
```

Exercise 6.5 Call-By- Reference (continued).

In Exercise 6.5, the first two dates are initialized with different values as **local** variables in the **main** function. The **swapper** function swaps those two dates. It accepts two **date** references and swaps them by using simple assignment statements. Because the parameters are references, the swapping occurs to the **main** function's copy of the structures.

Exercise 6.5 displays the following date formats:

```
Now:   23/2/90
Then:  10/9/60
Now:   10/9/60
Then:  23/2/90
```

When Not to Use References

Consider again Exercise 6.5. The call in **main** to **swapper** gives no indication that it uses references. The compiler knows to use references because that is how the function is prototyped and declared. But the programmer who writes **main** might not know that.

Given the purpose of the **swapper** function, it should be obvious that it uses references. If it did not, it would swap its own copies of the parameters, accomplishing nothing. But it might not be so obvious that other functions could change a caller's copy of a parameter. If the prototype is in a header file and the function is in an object library or a separately compiled source module, the reader gets no clue from the code about what is going to happen when the function gets called.

In cases like this, you can use pointers for parameters where the called function is going to modify the caller's copy of the variable. If the calling code does not pass the address of the parameter, the reader can assume that the function does not modify the parameter. If the call passes an address, the reader sees that the parameter might be changed. The first assumption is valid only if the reader knows about the coding convention that is suggested here and if the programmer always complies with it. Nothing in C++ prevents you from disregarding such conventions and not telling anybody.

const Reference Parameters

You can qualify unmodifiable reference function parameters by using the **const** qualifer. A function that accepts a reference to a **const** as a parameter cannot modify the referenced object. This notation is shown here:

```
void foo(const Date& dt); // foo cannot modify dt
```

This practice assures the caller that the variable is unchanged when the function returns.

Returning a Reference

You have seen how you can pass a reference to a function as a parameter. You can also return a reference from a function. When a function returns a reference, the function call can exist in any context where a reference can exist, including on the receiving side of an assignment.

Exercise 6.6 calls a function to select from an array of dates.

```
#include <iostream.h>
#include <stdlib.h>

// ---------- a date structure
struct Date {
    int mo, da, yr;
};

// -------- an array of dates
Date birthdays[] = {
    {12, 17, 37},
    {10, 31, 38},
    { 6, 24, 40},
    {11, 23, 42},
    { 8,  5, 44},
};

// ----- a function to retrieve a date
Date& getdate(int n)
{
    return birthdays[n-1];
}
```

Exercise 6.6 Returning a Reference from a Function.

```
main(int argc, char *argv[])
{
    if (argc > 1)    {
        Date& bd = getdate(atoi(argv[1]));
        cout << bd.mo << '/' << bd.da << '/' << bd.yr;
    }
}
```

Exercise 6.6 Returning a Reference from a Function (continued).

Exercise 6.6 displays a different date depending on the command line option, which must be 1–5. Following are the messages displayed on a PC. The first line of each pair is the MS-DOS command line prompt and the program command you enter. The second line is the date that the exercise displays.

```
C>ex06006 1
12/17/37
C>ex06006 2
10/31/38
C>ex06006 3
6/24/40
C>ex06006 4
11/23/42
C>ex06006 5
8/5/44
```

You must not return a reference to an automatic variable. The code in the following example may not work proprely:

```
date& getdate(void)
{
    date dt = {6, 24, 40};
    return dt;   // bad-reference to auto variable
}
```

The problem is that the **dt** variable goes out of scope when the function returns. You would, therefore, be returning a reference to a variable that no longer exists, and the calling program would be referring to a date that does not exist. Some C++ compilers issue a warning when they see code that returns references to automatic variables. If you ignore the warning, you get unpredictable results. Sometimes the program appears to work because the stack location where the automatic variable existed is intact when the reference is used. A program that appears to work in some cases can fail in others due to device or multitasking interrupts that use the stack.

Note that a program that calls a function that returns a variable might not know whether the function returns a whole variable or a reference. The compiler makes the determination and generates appropriate code in either case.

Things You Cannot Do with References

There is a tendency among C++ programmers who are making the transition from C to think of references as pointer forms rather than aliases. Here again is the list of things that you cannot do to a reference.

- Point to Them
- Have an Array of Them
- Take the Address of One
- Compare Them
- Assign to Them
- Do arithmetic to Them
- Modify Them

When you try to do one of these things, you might think you are getting away with it because the compiler does not complain. Chances are the operation you are trying to apply to the reference is being applied to what the reference refers to. If you try to increment a reference, you increment what it refers to if its data type accepts the increment operator. If you take the address of a reference, you are really taking the address of what the reference refers to.

All you can do with the reference itself is initialize it. Everything else is done to what the reference refers to, not to the reference.

Summary

The reference is a handy way to optimize your program by eliminating the overhead associated with moving large structures around in memory. You will use the reference variable extensively after you learn to build C++ classes in the next chapter. Later, when you learn about operator overloading, you will see more uses for the reference.

Classes

Before coming up with its present name, Dr. Stroustrup called C++, "C with classes." Classes support the way you use C++ for object-oriented programming, and they are the way you build new data types into the language. These two activities have a lot in common.

You will learn more about object-oriented programming in Chapter 13. For now, however, think of classes as the means for extending C++ by designing and implementing new data types. You will learn about:

- Designing a class
- Data members
- Member functions
- Constructors and destructors
- Class conversion functions
- Friends
- References
- Assignment functions
- The this pointer
- Arrays of class objects
- Static class members
- The free store
- Copy constructors

The Class

Consider the intrinsic numerical data types that C and C++ use. There are several types of integer and floating-point numbers. These suffice for most of your numerical needs, but there are times when the basic types need to be expanded. In C you would traditionally organize the basic types into a logical structure and write functions to manipulate that structure. With C++ you do the same thing but you also bind the data description and its algorithms together and set them up as a new data type by defining a class. The class in C++ is a data type defined by the programmer. The class consists of a user-defined data structure, member functions, and, as you will learn in Chapter 8, custom operators.

Class Definition

A class resembles the structure you learned about in Chapter 5. The class is distinguished from the C structure by its ability to hide some of its members from the rest of the program. Exercise 7.1 is an example of a class that describes the geometrical cube form.

 Before proceeding to Exercise 7.1 ask yourself why you might want to build a class that describes a cube. Perhaps you are writing a program that deals with cubic containers of one kind or another, and the cube is a basic unit that the program must deal with. Any data entity that your program might process is a candidate to be a class in C++. This begins to answer the question, "What are the objects?", which is posed in Chapter 13.

Exercise 7.1 introduces classes by defining the **Cube** class.

```
#include <iostream.h>

// ----------- a Cube class
class Cube    {
private:
    int height, width, depth;    // private data members
public:
    Cube(int, int, int); // constructor function
    ~Cube();            // destructor function
    int volume();        // member function (compute volume)
};
// ---------- the constructor function
Cube::Cube(int ht, int wd, int dp)
{
    height - ht;
    width - wd;
    depth - dp;
}
// ---------- the destructor function
Cube::~Cube()
{
    // does nothing
}
// -------- member function to compute the Cube's volume
int Cube::volume()
{
    return height * width * depth;
}
```

*Exercise 7.1 The **Cube** Class.*

```
//  ========= an application to use the cube
main()
{
    Cube thiscube(7, 8, 9);      // declare a Cube
    cout << thiscube.volume();   // compute & display volume
}
```

*Exercise 7.1 The **Cube** Class (continued).*

Exercise 7.1 displays the cube's volume, which is 504.

There are a lot of new C++ features packed into Exercise 7.1. The program begins by defining the **Cube** class. The **Cube** has three private data members, the integers **height**, **width**, and **depth**, and three public functions: the constructor, **Cube**; the destructor, **~Cube**; and the member function, **volume**.

Class Declaration

As just shown, class definition only defines the class; it does not set aside any memory to hold any instance of the class. No instance of the class exists until a program declares one. This definition/declaration relationship is the same as that of a C structure. Exercise 7.1 declares an instance of the **Cube** class named **thiscube** in the **main** function. An instance of a class is called an *object*. Therefore, **thiscube** is an object of type **Cube**.

The declaration of a class object can contain a list of initializers in parentheses. The declaration of **thiscube** contains three integer values. These values are passed to the class's constructor function, described soon.

Class Members

A class is a souped-up structure. As such, it has members, just as a structure does. A class's members are defined in the class's definition and consist of data members, the constructor and destructor functions, and member functions.

Class member visibility

The **private** and **public** access specifiers in the class definition specify the visibility of the members that follow the access specifiers. The mode invoked by an access specifier continues until another access specifier occurs or the class definition ends. Private members can be accessed only by member functions. Public members can be accessed by member functions and by other functions that declare an instance of the class. There are exceptions to these general rules. The discussion on the **friend** class and function later in this chapter addresses those exceptions.

The **Cube** class, therefore, specifies that its three integer data members are visible only to the constructor and destructor functions and to the **volume** member function, all three of which are visible to outside functions. You can use the **private** and **public** access specifiers as often as you want in a class definition, but many programmers group the **private** and **public** members separately.

All class definitions begin with the **private** access specifier as the default mode, so you could omit it in Exercise 7.1. The exercise includes it for readability and to demonstrate its purpose. However, that point introduces what might come as a surprise. Chapter 5 discussed C++ structures but only briefly, deferring the more complicated subjects for this chapter. The surprise is that there are only a few small differences between the structure and the class. First, the structure begins with **public** access as the default, and the class begins with the **private** access as the default. Second, if the structure is derived from a base class, the base class is public by default. If the class is derived from a base class, the base class is private by default. You have already learned about access specifiers. Chapter 9 discusses public and private base classes and class derivation—inheritance—in general. Many programmers adopt a style where they define a structure when its form complies with the C definition of a structure. Otherwise, they define a class.

A third access specifier, the **protected** keyword, works the same as the **private** keyword except when you use class inheritance. For now, you do not use the **protected** access specifier.

Exercise 7.1 shows the convention that many C++ programmers follow. When designing a class, make the data members **private** and the member functions **public**. If you need to view or modify a **private** data value, do it with a **public** member function set up for that purpose. This convention is not a rule, and there are times when you find it necessary to do otherwise. But if you use the convention as a guideline, your programs are more object oriented.

Data members

The data members of the class are the ones that are data types. A data member may be any valid C++ data type including an instance of another class. The **Cube** class has three data members, the integers **height**, **width**, and **depth**.

Initialization

You initialize a class object with a constructor function, which is discussed later in this chapter. However, if the class has no private or protected members, no **virtual** functions (defined later), and is not derived from another class, you can initialize an object of the class with a brace-delimited, comma-separated, list of initializers, just like you initialize C structures, as shown here:

```
class Date  {
public:
    int mo, da, yr;
};

main()
{
    Date dt = {1,29,92};
}
```

The same restrictions apply to structures, by the way. You cannot use a brace-delimited initializer list if a structure has any of the attributes just mentioned.

Member functions

The member functions of the class are the functions that are declared within the class definition. You must provide the code for these functions just as you did for the functions in structures in Chapter 5.

There are several categories of member functions. The constructor and destructor, discussed soon, are two of them. The others are member functions, which are regular members of the class, or **friend**, **virtual**, or **static** functions. You will learn about **friend**, **virtual**, and **static** functions later. For now, note that the **Cube** class has one member function, named **volume**, which is neither **friend** nor **virtual**. Member functions are named with the class name followed by the **::** operator followed by the function name. The name of the **Cube** class's **volume** member function is, therefore, **Cube::volume**.

The **Cube::volume** function returns the product of the **Cube**'s three dimensions. The program in Exercise 7.1 calls the **volume** function by using the same convention for calling a structure's function. Use structure member notation with the period operator as illustrated in the following example:

```
int vol = thiscube.volume();
```

You can call the **volume** member function anywhere an object of type **Cube** is in scope. Member functions of a class can call one another as well by using the function name without the object name prefix. The compiler assumes that the call is being made for the same object that the calling member function was called for.

When a member function is **private**, only other member functions within the same class can call it.

The Scope of a Class Object

A class object is like any other data type with respect to scope. It comes into scope when the program declares it, and it goes out of scope when the program exits the block in which the class object is declared.

An **extern** class object comes into scope when the program begins and goes out of scope when the program ends.

If you give a local class object the **static** keyword, its scope is the same as an **automatic** object, but its actual existence is the same duration as that of an **extern** object. This becomes a matter to consider because C++ classes involve those special functions called the **constructor** and **destructor** functions.

inline Functions

A class can have **inline** functions. You learned about regular **inline** functions in Chapter 2. The same guidelines apply when you decide whether a class member function should be **inline**. **Inline** functions should be small.

There is a special notation for defining **inline** functions for a class. You code the body of the function directly into the class definition rather than coding a prototype. Both the **Cube** constructor function and the **Cube**'s **volume** member function are small enough to be **inline** functions. By coding them as **inline** and removing the unnecessary destructor function, you can significantly reduce the size of the program's source code.

Exercise 7.2 illustrates a class member function coded to be an **inline** member function.

```
#include <iostream.h>

// ------------ a Cube class
class Cube    {
    int height, width, depth;      // private data members
public:
    // ------ inline constructor function
    Cube(int ht, int wd, int dp)
        { height = ht; width = wd; depth = dp; }
    // ----- inline member function
    int volume()
        { return height * width * depth; }
};

main()
{
    Cube thiscube(7, 8, 9);      // declare a Cube
    cout << thiscube.volume();   // compute & display volume
}
```

*Exercise 7.2 The **Cube** Class with **inline** Functions.*

Exercise 7.2 displays the **cube**'s volume, which is 504.

You often see **inline** class functions coded on a single line. This convention reinforces the idea that **inline** functions should be small. If you cannot get the function's body on a single line, then perhaps the function should not be an **inline** one.

Constructors

When an instance of a class comes into scope, a special function called the constructor executes. It does, that is, if you have defined one. You declare the constructor when you define the class. The **Cube** class has a constructor function named **Cube**. Constructor functions always have the same name as the class, and they specify no return value, not even **void**.

The run-time system provides enough memory to contain the data members of a class when the class object comes into scope. The system does not necessarily initialize the data members. The class's constructor function must do any initialization that the class requires. The data variable memory returns to the system when the object goes out of scope.

The constructor function initializes the class object. The **Cube** constructor function in Exercise 7.2 accepts three integer parameters and uses these parameters to load the data members with values that describe the **Cube**.

Observe the declaration of **thiscube** in Exercise 7.2. It follows the C syntax for declaring a variable. First comes the data type—Cube in this case—then comes the name of the object, **thiscube**. That's the same way you would declare an **int**, for example. But the declaration of a class object can contain an argument list in parentheses as well. This list represents class object initializers and contains the arguments that are passed to the constructor function. There must be a constructor function in the class definition with a parameter list of data types that match those of the argument list in the class object declaration.

If the constructor function has an empty parameter list, the declaration of the object does not include the parentheses.

A constructor function returns nothing. You do not declare it as void.

You may define multiple, overloaded constructor functions for a class. Each of these would have a distinct parameter list. More discussion of this feature follows later.

Constructors with Default Arguments

Perhaps you want to initialize a **Cube** with dimensions as you did in Exercise 7.1, but at other times you want a **Cube** with default dimensions.

Exercise 7.3 shows a **Cube** class that defaults to specified dimensions if you do not supply initializers.

```
#include <iostream.h>

// ------------ a Cube class
class Cube    {
    int height, width, depth;    // private data members
public:
    // ----- constructor function with default initializers
    Cube(int ht = 1, int wd = 2, int dp = 3)
        { height = ht; width = wd; depth = dp; }
    // ----- member function
    int volume() { return height * width * depth; }
};

main()
{
    Cube thiscube(7, 8, 9);    // declare a Cube
    Cube defaultcube;          // no initializers
    cout << thiscube.volume(); // volume of the Cube
    cout << '\n';
    cout << defaultcube.volume(); // volume of the default
}
```

Exercise 7.3 Constructor with Default Parameters.

Exercise 7.3 displays the initialized **Cube**'s volume, which is 504, followed by the default **Cube**'s volume, which is 6.

Overloaded Constructors

A class can have more than one constructor function. The several constructor functions for a class must have different parameter lists with respect to the number and types of parameters so the compiler can tell them apart. You would code multiple constructors in cases where the declarations of a class can occur with different initialization parameters. Perhaps you want to initialize a **Cube** with dimensions as you did in Exercise 7.1, but at other times you simply want an empty **Cube** with no initial dimensions; for example, to be on the receiving end of an assignment.

Exercise 7.4 shows the **Cube** with two constructor functions.

```cpp
#include <iostream.h>

// ----------- a Cube class
class Cube    {
    int height, width, depth;      // private data members
public:
    // ------ constructor functions
    Cube() { /* does nothing */ }
    Cube(int ht, int wd, int dp)
        { height = ht; width = wd; depth = dp; }
    // ----- member function
    int volume() { return height * width * depth; }
};

main()
{
    Cube thiscube(7, 8, 9);     // declare a Cube
    Cube othercube;             // a Cube with no initializers
    othercube = thiscube;
    cout << othercube.volume();
}
```

Exercise 7.4 A Class with Two Constructors.

Exercise 7.4 displays the **Cube**'s volume, which is 504, on the screen.

This exercise uses the simplest of differences between constructors where one constructor has initializers and the other one does not. The differences between constructors can be much greater depending on the types of the class's data members and the algorithms that associate with the constructor function. You will see more complex constructor functions in later chapters.

Class Conversions

Use of C++ data types involves the implicit application of type conversion rules. If you use an **int** expression where the compiler expects a **long** variable, for example, the compiler invokes one of the type conversion rules to convert the original integer value to the new **long** format. Such conversions already exist for all pairs of data types that are compatible with respect to conversions. These implicit conversions come into play in assignments, function arguments, return values, initializers, and expressions.

Conversion Functions

You can build the same kind of implicit conversions into your classes by building conversion functions. When you write a function that converts any data type to a class, you tell the compiler to use the conversion function when the syntax of a statement implies that the conversion should take effect; that is, when the compiler expects an object of the class and sees the other data type instead.

There are two ways to write a conversion function. The first is to write a special constructor function; the second is to write a member conversion function.

Conversion constructors

A constructor function that has only one entry in its parameter list is a conversion constructor. It works in the usual way as a constructor when you declare an object of the class type with a matching initializer argument. It is a conversion constructor if you use the argument type in the syntax where the class type is expected.

You use the constructor conversion function to convert from a different data type to the class in which you define the constructor conversion function.

These exercises use the **Date** class that stores its values as an integer for each of the elements month, day, and year.

Exercise 7.5 demonstrates a constructor conversion function that converts the value returned by the standard **time** function to the **Date** class.

```
#include <iostream.h>
#include <time.h>

class Date {
    int mo, da, yr;
public:
    Date() {}          // null constructor
    Date(time_t);      // constructor conversion function
    void display();
};
// ----- member function to display the date
void Date::display()
{
    cout << mo << '/' << da << '/' << yr;
}
// ------ constructor conversion function
Date::Date(time_t now)
{
    struct tm *tim = localtime(&now);
    da = tim->tm_mday;
    mo = tim->tm_mon + 1;
    yr = tim->tm_year;
}

main()
{
    time_t now = time(0); // today's date and time
    Date dt(now);      // invoke the conversion constructor
    dt.display();      // display today's date
}
```

Exercise 7.5 Constructor Conversion Function.

Exercise 7.5 displays the current date in month/day/year format, for example, 5/3/91.

Member conversion functions

You use a member conversion function to convert from the class in which you define it to a different data type. A member conversion function uses the C++ **operator** keyword in its declaration. This usage is an early exposure to C++ **operator** overloading in classes, the subject of Chapter 8. To declare a member conversion function within a class, you code its prototype as illustrated by the following example:

```
operator long();
```

The **long** in this example is the type specifier of the converted data type. The type specifier can be any valid C++ type, including another class. You would define the member conversion function with the following notation:

```
Classname::operator long()
```

The **Classname** identifier is the type specifier of the class in which the function is declared and from which you convert to get the **long**. The function must return the data type to which it is converting, in this case a **long**.

There is not enough information in the **Date** class to convert it back to the **time_t** variable, but you can convert it to, for example, a **long** integer containing the number of days since the beginning of the century.

Exercise 7.6 shows how you would use a member function to make the conversion.

```
#include <iostream.h>

class Date {
    int mo, da, yr;
public:
    Date(int m, int d, int y) { mo = m; da = d; yr = y; }
```

Exercise 7.6 Conversion Member Function.

```
        operator long();     // member conversion function
};

// ---- the member conversion function
Date::operator long()
{
    static int dys[]={31,28,31,30,31,30,31,31,30,31,30,31};
    long days = yr;
    days *= 365;
    days += yr / 4;
    for (int i = 0; i < mo-1; i++)
        days += dys[i];
    days += da;
    return days;
}

main()
{
    Date xmas(12, 25, 89);
    long since = xmas;
    cout << '\n' << since;
}
```

Exercise 7.6 Conversion Member Function (continued).

Exercise 7.6 displays the number 32866, which is the number of days from the turn of the century until Christmas of 1989.

Converting Classes

The conversion examples so far have converted a class to and from a fixed C++ data type. You can also define conversion functions that convert from one class to another.

Exercise 7.7 shows you how to convert classes.

```cpp
#include <iostream.h>

// -------- Julian date class
class Julian {
public:
    int da, yr;
    Julian() {}
    Julian(int d, int y) { da = d; yr = y;}
    void display(){ cout << '\n' << yr << '-' << da; }
};

// ------- date class
class Date {
    int mo, da, yr;
public:
    Date() {}
    Date(int m, int d, int y) { mo = m; da = d; yr = y; }
    Date(Julian);          // constructor conversion function
    operator Julian();     // member conversion function
    void display(){cout << '\n' << mo << '/' << da
                    << '/' << yr;}
};
static int dys[] = {31,28,31,30,31,30,31,31,30,31,30,31};

// -- constructor conversion function (Date <- Julian)
Date::Date(Julian jd)
{
```

Exercise 7.7 Converting Classes.

```
    yr = jd.yr;
    da = jd.da;
    for (mo = 0; mo < 11; mo++)
        if (da > dys[mo])
            da -= dys[mo];
        else
            break;
    mo++;
}


// ---- member conversion function (Julian <- Date)
Date::operator Julian()
{
    Julian jd(0, yr);
    for (int i = 0; i < mo-1; i++)
        jd.da += dys[i];
    jd.da += da;
    return jd;
}


main()
{
    Date dt(11,17,89);
    Julian jd;
    // ------- convert Date to Julian
    jd = dt;
    jd.display();
    // ------- convert Julian to Date
    dt = jd;
    dt.display();
}
```

Exercise 7.7 Converting Classes (continued).

Exercise 7.7 displays the two converted date formats as shown here.

89-321

11/17/89

This exercise has two classes, a **Julian** date and a **Date**. A **Julian** date is one that contains the year and the day of the year from 1 to 365. The conversion functions in Exercise 7.7 convert between the two date formats.

The date conversion algorithms in these exercises do not consider things such as the millennium or the leap year. These omissions are intentional to keep the exercises as simple as possible.

Both kinds of conversion functions are built into the **Date** class in Exercise 7.7. This approach works because you convert from the **Date** type to the **Julian** type with the member conversion function and from the **Julian** type to the **Date** type with the constructor conversion function.

Note that it would not be legal to have a **Date** to **Julian** member conversion function in the **Date** class and a **Date** to **Julian** constructor conversion function in the **Julian** class. The compiler would not know which function to call to perform the conversion and would issue an error.

Invoking Conversion Functions

There are three C++ forms that invoke a conversion function. The first is implicit conversion. For example, where the compiler expects to see a **Date** and the program supplies a **Julian**, the compiler calls the appropriate conversion function. The other two forms involve explicit conversions that you write into the code. The first of these conversions is implied by the C++ cast. The second is an explicit call to the conversion constructor or member conversion function.

Exercise 7.8 illustrates the three class conversion forms.

```
#include <iostream.h>

// -------- Julian date class
class Julian {
public:
    int da, yr;
    Julian() {}
    Julian(int d, int y) { da = d; yr = y;}
    void display(){cout << '\n' << yr << '-' << da;}
};

// ------- date class
class Date {
    int mo, da, yr;
public:
    Date(int m, int d, int y) { mo = m; da = d; yr = y; }
    operator Julian(); // conversion function
};

static int dys[] = {31,28,31,30,31,30,31,31,30,31,30,31};

// ---- member conversion function (Julian <- Date)
Date::operator Julian()
{
    Julian jd(0, yr);
    for (int i = 0; i < mo-1; i++)
        jd.da += dys[i];
    jd.da += da;
    return jd;
}
main()
```

Exercise 7.8 Invoking Conversions.

```
{
    Date dt(11,17,89);
    Julian jd;
    // ------- implicit conversion
    jd = dt;
    jd.display();
    // ------- convert Date to Julian via cast
    jd = (Julian) dt;
    jd.display();
    // ------- call the conversion function
    jd = Julian(dt);
    jd.display();
}
```

Exercise 7.8 Invoking Conversions (continued).

Exercise 7.8 displays the three **Julian** dates that were converted from conventional dates in three ways as shown here:

```
89-321
89-321
89-321
```

The Contexts Where Conversions Occur

So far the exercises have invoked conversion functions through assignment. The following list identifies several other contexts in which a conversion function comes into play:

- As a function argument
- As an initializer
- As a return value
- In an expression

Exercise 7.9 illustrates some of the ways you can cause a conversion function to be called.

```
#include <iostream.h>

// -------- Julian date class
class Julian {
public:
    int da, yr;
    Julian() {}
    Julian(int d, int y) { da = d; yr = y;}
    void display(){cout << '\n' << yr << '-' << da;}
};


// ------- date class
class Date {
    int mo, da, yr;
public:
    Date(int m, int d, int y) { mo = m; da = d; yr = y; }
    operator Julian(); // conversion function
};
// ----- a class that expects a Julian date as an initializer
class Tester {
    Julian jd;
public:
    Tester(Julian j) { jd = j; }
    void display() { jd.display(); }
};

static int dys[] = {31,28,31,30,31,30,31,31,30,31,30,31};
```

Exercise 7.9 Contexts for Conversions.

```
// ---- member conversion function (Julian <- Date)
Date::operator Julian()
{
    Julian jd(0, yr);
    for (int i = 0; i < mo-1; i++)
        jd.da += dys[i];
    jd.da += da;
    return jd;
}

// -------- a function that expects a Julian date
void dispdate(Julian jd)
{
    jd.display();
}

// --------- a function that returns a Julian Date
Julian rtndate()
{
    Date dt(10,11,88);
    return dt;        // this will be converted to Julian
}

main()
{
    Date dt(11,17,89);
    Julian jd;
    // ------- convert Date to Julian via assignment
    jd = dt;
    jd.display();
```

Exercise 7.9 Contexts for Conversions (continued).

```
    // ---- convert Date to Julian via function argument
    dispdate(dt);
    // ------- convert Date to Julian via initializer
    Tester ts(dt);
    ts.display();
    // ------- convert Date to Julian via return value
    jd = rtndate();
    jd.display();
}
```

Exercise 7.9 Contexts for Conversions (continued).

Exercise 7.9 displays the **Julian** dates converted from four different program contexts as shown here:

89-321

89-321

89-321

88-284

Conversion within an expression occurs in those expressions where one type is expected and another type is found. This process is better illustrated when the conversion is to a numeric type instead of another class.

Exercise 7.10 uses the earlier conversion of a date to a **long** integer to illustrate how the integral representation of a class can, through conversion, contribute directly to an expression.

```
#include <iostream.h>

class Date {
    int mo, da, yr;
public:
    Date(int m, int d, int y) { mo = m; da = d; yr = y; }
    operator long();    // member conversion function
};

// ---- the member conversion function
Date::operator long()
{
    static int dys[]={31,28,31,30,31,30,31,31,30,31,30,31};
    long days = yr;
    days *= 365;
    days += yr / 4;
    for (int i = 0; i < mo-1; i++)
        days += dys[i];
    days += da;
    return days;
}
main()
{
    Date today(2, 12, 90);
    const long ott = 123;
    long sum = ott + today;    // today is converted to long
    cout << ott << " + " << (long) today << " = " << sum;
}
```

Exercise 7.10 Conversion in an Expression.

Exercise 7.10 displays this expression:

```
123 + 32915 = 33038
```

The implicit conversion from within an expression occurs for a class-to-class conversion if the converted class can appear in a conversion; that is, if the converted class can itself be converted to a numerical type, or if the expression invokes an overloaded operator that works with the class. Chapter 8 discusses overloading operators.

Manipulating Private Data Members

All of the data members in the **Julian** class in Exercises 7.7, 7.8, and 7.9 are public. This approach allows the conversion functions in the **Date** class to read and write the data members of the **Julian** object. Making the members public is one way to allow this access, but when you do, you make the members public to all other functions as well. You might not want to do that. Remember the convention for keeping the data members **private** and the member functions **public**. These exercises violated that convention to get their point across. Now you should consider alternative ways to get the same results within the bounds of the accepted conventions.

As a general rule, you make all of the data members **private** and you provide member functions to read and write them.

Exercise 7.11 shows how the **Date** class can have member functions that provide controlled access to the data members.

```
#include <iostream.h>

class Date {
    int mo, da, yr;
public:
    Date(int m, int d, int y) { mo = m; da = d; yr = y; }
    // ---- a member function to return the year
    int getyear() { return yr; }
    // ---- a member function to allow the year to be changed
    int& year() { return yr; }
};

main()
{
    // -------- set up a Date
    Date dt(4, 1, 89);
    // ------- use a member function to read the year value
    cout << "\nThe year is: " << dt.getyear();
    // ------ use a member function to change the year
    dt.year() = 90;
    cout << "\nThe new year is: " << dt.getyear();
}
```

Exercise 7.11 Manipulating Data Members Though Member Functions.

Exercise 7.11 displays these messages:

```
The year is: 89
The new year is: 90
```

By consistently using this approach, you ensure that accesses and changes to the data of a class are managed by the member functions that are bound to the class. This binding strengthens a software design and makes it easier to maintain.

Now, to continue, Exercise 7.12 uses the member function access technique to improve the code in the conversion function that converts a **Date** object to a **Julian** object.

```
#include <iostream.h>

// -------- Julian date class
class Julian {
    int da, yr;
public:
    Julian() {}
    Julian(int d, int y) { da = d; yr = y;}
    void display(){cout << '\n' << yr << '-' << da;}
    // ------ member function to read and write a day
    int& day() { return da; }
};

// ------- date class
class Date {
    int mo, da, yr;
public:
    Date(int m, int d, int y) { mo = m; da = d; yr = y; }
    operator Julian(); // conversion function
};

static int dys[] = {31,28,31,30,31,30,31,31,30,31,30,31};
// ---- member conversion function (Julian <- Date)
Date::operator Julian()
{
```

Exercise 7.12 Conversions with Proper Data Hiding.

```
        Julian jd(0, yr);
        for (int i = 0; i < mo-1; i++)
            jd.day() += dys[i];        // uses member function to
        jd.day() += da;               // change da in Julian class
        return jd;
    }
main()
{
    Date dt(11,17,89);
    Julian jd;
    // ------- convert Date to Julian via assignment
    jd = dt;
    jd.display();
}
```

Exercise 7.12 Conversions with Proper Data Hiding (continued).

Exercise 7.12 displays this converted **Julian Date**:

```
89-321
```

Restricting Access to Data Members

Observe that the **year** member function in Exercise 7.11 and the **day** member function in Exercise 7.12 return references. Because each function returns a reference, you can use the function call on the left side of an assignment the way the exercises show. This practice, however, compromises one of the principles of object-oriented design. It permits the using program to directly modify the value of a data member, thereby binding the user to the implementation of the class. A better way is to provide two member functions for the data member, one that returns its current value and one that accepts a new value with which to modify it as shown here:

```
// ---- a member function to return the year
int getyear() { return yr; }
// ---- a member function to allow the year to be changed
void change_year(int y) { yr = y; }
```

This practice allows the class designer to change the implementation without affecting the code of the users.

There are valid uses of the reference return, and you will learn about some of them in Chapter 8.

const Member Functions

You can insure that a member function never modifies the object for which it is called by declaring it with the **const** qualifier as shown here:

```
// ---- a member function to return the year
int getyear() const;
```

No change to the **Date::getyear** function is permitted to modify the data members in the object. This is a way to insure that the member function's only purpose is to retrieve data values from the object.

Friends

Having learned that hidden access to data members is best, you must now consider the exceptions to that rule. There are times when a class definition must allow outside functions to directly read and write the class's data members.

As an example, the technique you just learned involves calling a function every time you want access to a particular data member of a class. The member functions that granted the access in the exercises were **inline** functions, so the overhead involved in their use is minimal. But if such an access requires enough processing that an **inline** function is impractical, then each read or write of a data member involves the overhead associated with a call to a function. In this case, you could encode the accessing function as a **friend** to the class where the data item is a member.

The **friend** keyword in a class specifies that a function or all of the member functions of another class can read and write the original class's private data members.

Friend Classes

The first kind of **friend** is the class **friend**. A class can specify that all of the member functions of another class can read and write the first class's private data members by identifying the other class as a **friend**.

Exercise 7.13 illustrates the use of the **friend** class.

```
#include <iostream.h>

class Date;        // tells compiler a Date class is coming
// -------- Julian date class
class Julian {
    int da, yr;
public:
    Julian() {}
    Julian(int d, int y) { da = d; yr = y;}
    void display() {cout << '\n' << yr << '-' << da;}
    friend Date;    // allows Date member functions to see
                    // Julian private members
};
// ------- date class
class Date {
    int mo, da, yr;
public:
    Date(int m, int d, int y) { mo = m; da = d; yr = y; }
    operator Julian();
};
```

Exercise 7.13 ***Friend*** *Classes.*

```
static int dys[] = {31,28,31,30,31,30,31,31,30,31,30,31};

// ---- member conversion function (Julian <- Date)
Date::operator Julian()
{
    Julian jd(0, yr);
    for (int i = 0; i < mo-1; i++)
        jd.da += dys[i];
    jd.da += da;
    return jd;
}

main()
{
    Date dt(11,17,89);
    Julian jd;
    jd = dt;
    jd.display();
}
```

Exercise 7.13 **Friend** *Classes (continued).*

Exercise 7.13 displays this converted **Julian Date**:

```
89-321
```

Observe this new construct in the **Julian** class of Exercise 7.13 in the following example:

```
friend Date;
```

This statement tells the compiler that member functions of the **Date** class have access to the private members of the **Julian** class. The conversion functions of the **Date** class need to see the individual data components of the **Julian** class, and so the entire **Date** class is named as a **friend** of the **Julian** class.

Another new C++ construct is contained in Exercise 7-13. The beginning of the program has the following statement:

```
class Date;
```

This statement tells the compiler that a class named **Date** is defined later. The compiler needs to know about that because the **Julian** class refers to the **Date** class, and the **Date** class refers to the **Julian** class. One of them must come first, so the statement serves to resolve the forward reference to **Date** that occurs in the **Julian** class.

You can eliminate the need for the **class Date;** statement by including the **class** keyword in the friend declaration.

Exercise 7.14 modifies the Exercise 7.13 program by using the **class** keyword.

```
#include <iostream.h>

// -------- Julian date class
class Julian {
    int da, yr;
public:
    Julian() {}
    Julian(int d, int y) { da = d; yr = y;}
    void display() {cout << '\n' << yr << '-' << da;}
    friend class Date;    // <- forward reference to class
};

// ------- date class
class Date {
    int mo, da, yr;
public:
    Date(int m, int d, int y) { mo = m; da = d; yr = y; }
    operator Julian();
};
```

*Exercise 7.14 **Friend** Classes, Forward Reference.*

```
static int dys[] = {31,28,31,30,31,30,31,31,30,31,30,31};

// ---- member conversion function (Julian <- Date)
Date::operator Julian()
{
    Julian jd(0, yr);
    for (int i = 0; i < mo-1; i++)
        jd.da += dys[i];
    jd.da += da;
    return jd;
}

main()
{
    Date dt(11,17,89);
    Julian jd;
    jd = dt;
    jd.display();
}
```

*Exercise 7.14 **Friend** Classes, Forward Reference (continued).*

Exercise 7.14 displays this converted **Julian Date**:

89-321

Friend Functions

Usually you do not want an entire class to be a **friend** of another class. Unless it is necessary to access data in such a broad way, then you should not do so. What you need is a way to specify that only selected member functions of another class may read and write the data members of the current class. In these cases, you may specify that a particular function rather than an entire class is a **friend** of a class.

Exercise 7.15 restricts the access to the data members of the **Julian** class to only the member function of the **Date** class that needs it.

```cpp
#include <iostream.h>

class Julian;
// ------- date class
class Date {
    int mo, da, yr;
public:
    Date() {}
    Date(Julian);          // constructor conversion function
    void display()
        {cout << '\n' << mo << '/' << da << '/' << yr;}
};
// -------- Julian date class
class Julian {
    int da, yr;
public:
    Julian(int d, int y) { da = d; yr = y; }
    friend Date::Date(Julian); // friend conversion function
};
static int dys[] = {31,28,31,30,31,30,31,31,30,31,30,31};
// ---- constructor conversion function (Date <- Julian)
Date::Date(Julian jd)
{
    yr = jd.yr;
    da = jd.da;
    for (mo = 0; mo < 11; mo++)
        if (da > dys[mo])
```

*Exercise 7.15 **Friend** Functions in a Class.*

```
                da -= dys[mo];
            else
                break;
        mo++;
    }
main()
{
    Date dt;
    Julian jd(123, 89);
    dt = jd;          // convert Julian to Date
    dt.display();
}
```

*Exercise 7.15 **Friend** Functions in a Class (continued).*

Exercise 7.15 displays this date converted from a **Julian Date**:

```
5/3/89
```

Sometimes the function that is to be a **friend** is not a member of another class at all. You may specify that a nonclass member function is a **friend** to a class. That function would then have the special privilege of reading and writing the class's private data members. This feature is particularly useful when overloading operators, the subject of Chapter 8.

A frequent use of nonmember **friend** functions is to bridge classes. A function that is **friend** to more than one class can have access to the private members of both. Suppose you have a **Time** class and a **Date** class and you want a function that displays both.

Exercise 7.16 shows how a **friend** function that has access to the data members of both classes can bridge the two.

```
#include <iostream.h>

class Time;

// ------- date class
class Date {
    int mo, da, yr;
public:
    Date(int m, int d, int y) { mo = m; da = d; yr = y;}
    friend void display(Date&, Time&); // bridge function
};

// ------- time class
class Time {
    int hr, min, sec;
public:
    Time(int h, int m, int s) { hr = h; min = m; sec = s;}
    friend void display(Date&, Time&); // bridge function
};

// -------- a bridge friend function
void display(Date& dt, Time& tm)
{
    cout << '\n' << dt.mo << '/' << dt.da << '/' << dt.yr;
    cout << ' ';
    cout << tm.hr << ':' << tm.min << ':' << tm.sec;
}
```

*Exercise 7.16 Bridging Classes with a **Friend** Function.*

```
main()
{
    Date dt(2,16,90);
    Time tm(10,55,0);
    display(dt, tm);
}
```

*Exercise 7.16 Bridging Classes with a **Friend** Function (continued).*

Exercise 7.16 displays this date and time message:

```
2/16/90 10:55:0
```

Destructors

When a class object goes out of scope, a special function called the **destructor** is called. You define the destructor when you define the class. The destructor function name is always that of the class with a tilde character (~) as a prefix.

There is only one destructor function for a class. A destructor function takes no parameters and returns nothing.

Until now, the exercises in this chapter have not treated the subject of destructors because the classes in them have not required anything in the way of custom destruction. Destructors are a peculiar breed of function with their own set of problems to consider.

The destructor function for the **Cube** class used earlier in this chapter does nothing. Exercise 7.1 included it to show its format. You could omit it altogether and get the same result. However, in other occasions destructors are necessary. For example, some classes allocate memory from the free store in their constructors. These classes use the destructors to return the memory to the free store.

To illustrate how destructors work, a new **Date** class includes a pointer to a string that contains the month spelled out. Exercise 7.17 shows the **destructor** function for the new **Date** class.

```
#include <iostream.h>
#include <string.h>

// ------- date class
class Date {
    int mo, da, yr;
    char *month;
public:
    Date();
    Date(int m, int d, int y);
    ~Date();
    void display();
};

// constructor that is called for an uninitialized Date
Date::Date()
{
    mo = 0; da = 0; yr = 0;
    month = 0;
}

// constructor that is called for an initialized Date
Date::Date(int m, int d, int y)
{
    static char *mos[] = {
        "January", "February", "March", "April", "May",
        "June", "July", "August", "September", "October",
        "November", "December"
    };
```

Exercise 7.17 Destructors.

```
        mo = m; da = d; yr = y;
        month = new char[strlen(mos[m-1])+1];
        strcpy(month, mos[m-1]);
    }


    // Destructor for a Date
    Date::~Date()
    {
        delete month;
    }
    // ----------- display member function
    void Date::display()
    {
        if (month != NULL)
            cout << '\n' << month << ' ' << da << ", "
                << yr+1900;
    }


    main()
    {
        Date birthday(6,24,40);
        birthday.display();
    }
```

Exercise 7.17 Destructors (continued).

Exercise 7.17 displays this date:

```
June 24, 1940
```

Note that as the member functions get bigger, they are no longer **inline** functions.

The constructor function for the uninitialized **Date** object sets all of the integer data members to zero and the **month** pointer to a null value.

The constructor function for the initialized **Date** object uses the **new** operator to allocate some free-store memory for the string name of the month. Then it copies the name from its internal array into the **Date** object's **month** character pointer. Of course, you could have simply copied the pointer from the constructor's array into the class in the context of this exercise, but the point of the exercise is to discuss destructors. If you had copied the pointer, the object would have nothing that needed destroying.

The destructor function deletes the **month** pointer if it contains a non-null value, and this is where you can get into trouble. As programmed, the exercise has no problems, but as designed, the **Date** class can cause trouble when used in an assignment. Suppose you added the following code to the main function in Exercise 7.17:

```
Date newday;
newday = birthday;9
```

You would construct an empty **Date** variable named **newday** and then assign the contents of **birthday** to it. That looks reasonable, but when you consider what the destructor function does, you see the problem.

C++ figures that if you do not tell it otherwise, a class assignment is either a binary copy or a member-by-member copy. In this example, the **birthday** variable has **month**, a character pointer that was initialized by the constructor's use of the **new** operator. The destructor uses the **delete** operator to release the memory when **birthday** goes out of scope. But when that happens **newday** goes out of scope too, and the destructor executes for it as well. The **month** pointer in **newday** is a copy of the **month** pointer in **birthday**. The constructor deletes the same pointer twice, giving unpredictable results, and that is a problem that you must deal with in your design of the class.

Furthermore, suppose that **newday** is an external object and **birthday** is automatic. When **birthday** goes out of scope, it deletes the **month** pointer in the **newday** object.

Now, suppose that you had two initialized **Date** variables and you assigned one to the other as in the following example:

```
Date birthday(6,24,40);
Date newday(7,29,41);
newday = birthday;
```

The problem compounds itself. When the two variables go out of scope, the **month** value originally assigned in **birthday** is in **newday** as a result of the assignment. The **month** value that the constructor's **new** operation put into **newday** has been overwritten by the assignment. Not only does the **month** value in **birthday** get deleted twice, the one that was originally in **newday** never gets deleted.

Class Assignment

The solution to the problems just posed lies in recognizing when they occur and writing a special assignment operator function to deal with them. The discussion on conversion functions earlier in this chapter introduced you to the technique for overloading the assignment operator to manage conversions between classes and other data types. You can overload the assignment operator for assigning two objects of the same class as well. It is with this technique that you solve the problem of assignment and destruction of free-store pointers in a class. (Chapter 8 discusses overloaded operators in detail.)

The technique you are about to learn is quite simple. Your class assignment function uses the new operator to get a different pointer from the free store. Then it copies the value pointed to in the assigning object, into the area pointed to in the assigned object.

Exercise 7.18 is an example of how the class-assignment technique works

```
#include <iostream.h>
#include <string.h>

// ------- date class
class Date {
    int mo, da, yr;
    char *month;
public:
    Date();
    Date(int m, int d, int y);
    ~Date();
    void operator=(Date&); // overloaded assignment operator
    void display();
};

// constructor that is called for an uninitialized Date
Date::Date()
{
    mo = 0; da = 0; yr = 0;
    month = 0;
}

// constructor that is called for an initialized Date
Date::Date(int m, int d, int y)
{
    static char *mos[] = {
        "January", "February", "March", "April", "May",
        "June", "July", "August", "September", "October",
        "November", "December"
    };
```

Exercise 7.18 Class Assignment.

```
    mo = m; da = d; yr = y;
    month = new char[strlen(mos[m-1])+1];
    strcpy(month, mos[m-1]);
}
// Destructor for a Date
Date::~Date()
{
    delete month;
}

// ----------- display member function
void Date::display()
{
    if (month != NULL)
        cout << '\n' << month << ' ' << da << ", "
            << yr+1900;
}

// ---------- overloaded Date assignment
void Date::operator=(Date& dt)
{
    mo = dt.mo;
    da = dt.da;
    yr = dt.yr;
    delete month;
    if (dt.month != 0)    {
        month = new char [strlen(dt.month)+1];
        strcpy(month, dt.month);
    }
    else
```

Exercise 7.18 Class Assignment (continued).

```
        month = 0;
}

main()
{
    // ------ first date
    Date birthday(6,24,40);
    birthday.display();
    // ------ second date
    Date newday(7,29,41);
    newday.display();
    // ------ assign first to second
    newday = birthday;
    newday.display();
}
```

Exercise 7.18 Class Assignment (continued).

This exercise contains all of the components of Exercise 7.17, but with the overloaded assignment operator function added to the **Date** class definition. The function makes the usual data-member assignments, then tests to see if the receiving object's **month** pointer has a non-null value. If so, the object has been initialized or previously assigned to, and, because of the assignment, its values are to be discarded. In that case, the function uses the **delete** operator to return the object's **month** string memory to the free store. Then, if the sending object's **month** pointer has been initialized (if not, the sender was never initialized), the function uses **new** to allocate memory for the receiving object and copies the sending object's **month** string to the receiver.

Exercise 7.18 displays the following messages:

```
June 24, 1940
July 29, 1941
June 24, 1940
```

You cannot always see the effects of the overloaded assignment function by observing a properly running program such as that in Exercise 7.18. The effects of leaving it out are different from compiler to compiler. In some cases, the code might even work for a time. The effects of deleting pointers that have already been deleted are undefined, and it is perfectly correct for the compiler to generate code that crashes if you do so. The effect of not deleting pointers that you no longer need is that you eventually exhaust the free store.

The *this* Pointer

The **this** pointer is a special pointer that exists for a class while a nonstatic member function is executing. The **this** pointer is a pointer to an object of the type of the class and it points to the object for which the member function is currently executing.

Note that **this** does not exist in a static member function (see the discussion on Static Members, later in this chapter).

When you call a member function for an object, the compiler assigns the address of the object to the **this** pointer and then calls the function. Therefore, every reference to a data member from within a member function implicitly uses the **this** pointer. The two output statements in the following example do the same thing.

In this example, the second statement explicitly uses the pointer notation that the first statement uses implicitly:

```
void Date::month_display()
{
    cout << mo;        // these two statements
    cout << this->mo; // do the same thing
}
```

Returning **this*

One purpose of the **this** pointer is to allow member functions to return the invoking object to the caller. The overloaded assignment operator function in

Exercise 7-18 returns nothing. With that function you would not be able to string assignments together in the C and C++ format as follows:

```
a = b = c;
```

Such an assignment works in C and C++ because every expression returns something, unless it is a function returning void. The preceding example can be expressed the following way:

```
b = c;
a = b;
```

Because the first statement is an expression that returns the value assigned, the two expressions can be combined as follows:

```
a = (b = c);
```

Because the rightmost assignment operator has higher precedence than the left-most one, the parentheses are not required, and the preceding example is thus expressed the following way:

```
a = b = c;
```

To make your overloaded class assignments work the same way, you must make the assignment function return the result of the assignment, which happens to be the object being assigned to. This also happens to be what the **this** pointer points to while the assignment function is executing.

Exercise 7.19 modifies Exercise 7-18 by having the overloaded assignment function return a reference to a **Date**. The value returned is the object pointed to by the **this** pointer.

```
#include <iostream.h>
#include <string.h>

// ------- date class
class Date {
    int mo, da, yr;
    char *month;
public:
    Date();
    Date(int m, int d, int y);
    ~Date();
    Date& operator=(Date&); //overloaded assignment operator
    void display();
};

// constructor that is called for an uninitialized Date
Date::Date()
{
    mo = 0; da = 0; yr = 0;
    month = 0;
}
// constructor that is called for an initialized Date
Date::Date(int m, int d, int y)
{
    static char *mos[] = {
        "January", "February", "March", "April", "May",
        "June", "July", "August", "September", "October",
        "November", "December"
    };
    mo = m; da = d; yr = y;
```

*Exercise 7.19 The **this** Pointer.*

```
        month = new char[strlen(mos[m-1])+1];
        strcpy(month, mos[m-1]);
    }
// Destructor for a Date
Date::~Date()
{
    delete month;
}


// ---------- display member function
void Date::display()
{
    if (month != 0)
        cout << '\n' << month << ' ' << da << ", "
            << yr+1900;
}


// ---------- overloaded Date assignment
Date& Date::operator=(Date& dt)
{
    mo = dt.mo;
    da = dt.da;
    yr = dt.yr;
    delete month;
    if (dt.month != 0)    {
        month = new char [strlen(dt.month)+1];
        strcpy(month, dt.month);
    }
    else
```

*Exercise 7.19 The **this** Pointer (continued).*

```
        month = 0;
    return *this;
}
main()
{
    // ------ original date
    Date birthday(6,24,40);
    Date oldday, newday;
    // ------ assign first to second to third
    oldday = newday = birthday;
    birthday.display();
    oldday.display();
    newday.display();
}
```

*Exercise 7.19 The **this** Pointer (continued).*

Exercise 7.19 displays these three dates:

```
June 24, 1940
June 24, 1940
June 24, 1940
```

This use of the **this** pointer is sometimes difficult to grasp because it applies several C++ constructs that are unfamiliar to the C programmer. Picture what is happening when you make the following assignment:

```
newday = birthday;
```

The assignment executes the overloaded assignment operator function for the **Date** class. That function has two parameters. The first parameter is implied. It is the address of the object for which the function is being called. In this case, the function is being called for the object on the left side of the assignment, the **newday** object. The second parameter is supplied as an argument and is the object on the right side of the assignment, in this case the **birthday** object. In the function, the **birthday** object becomes the **dt** parameter. The first statement in the function is as follows:

```
mo = dt.mo;
```

This statement can also be read the following way:

```
this->mo = dt.mo;
```

The statement assigns the value in the **mo** data member of the birthday object to the **mo** data member of the **newday** object. The other assignments work the same. When the function is done, it returns what **this** points to, the **newday** object. Because the function really returns a reference, the compiler converts the return of what **this** points to into a reference to what **this** points to. The result is that the overloaded assignment operator function, in addition to performing the assignment, returns the object that received the assignment making the following statement possible:

```
oldday = newday = birthday;
```

By understanding this mechanism and the subject of operator overloading (as discussed in Chapter 8), you can see how the chained **cout** statements used in previous exercises work. You have been using statements similar to the following example in many of the exercises.

```
cout << a << b << c;
```

Using *this* to Link Lists

The **this** pointer is convenient in applications where a data structure uses self-referential members. An example is the simple linked list.

Exercise 7.20 builds a linked list of a class named **ListEntry**.

```
#include <iostream.h>
#include <string.h>

class ListEntry {
    char *listvalue;
    ListEntry *preventry;
public:
    ListEntry(char *);
    ~ListEntry() { delete listvalue; }
    ListEntry *PrevEntry() { return preventry; };
    void display() { cout << '\n' << listvalue; }
    // ---------- use the 'this' pointer to chain the list
    void AddEntry(ListEntry& le) { le.preventry = this; }
};

ListEntry::ListEntry(char *s)
{
    listvalue = new char[strlen(s)+1];
    strcpy(listvalue, s);
    preventry = 0;
}

main()
{
    ListEntry *prev = 0;
    // ---------- read in some names
    while (1)    {
        cout << "\nEnter a name ('end' when done): ";
        char name[25];
        cin >> name;
```

Exercise 7.20 ***this*** *and the Linked List.*

```
        if (strncmp(name, "end", 3) == 0)
            break;
        // -------- make a list entry of the name
        ListEntry *list = new ListEntry(name);
        if (prev != 0)
            // -------- add the entry to the linked list
            prev->AddEntry(*list);
        prev = list;
    }
    // ------- display the names in reverse order
    while (prev != 0)    {
        prev->display();
        ListEntry *hold = prev;
        prev = prev->PrevEntry();
        // -------- delete the ListEntry
        delete hold;
    }
}
```

*Exercise 7.20 **this** and the Linked List (continued).*

Exercise 7.20 displays the following prompting messages. Enter names until you are done, then enter "end." The program displays the names in the reverse order in which you entered them.

```
Enter a name ('end' when done): Sonny
Enter a name ('end' when done): Jay
Enter a name ('end' when done): Alan
Enter a name ('end' when done): Wally
Enter a name ('end' when done): Julie
Enter a name ('end' when done): end
```

```
Julie
Wally
Alan
Jay
Sonny
```

The class in Exercise 7.20 has a string value and a pointer to the previous entry in the list. The constructor function gets memory for the string from the free store, copies the string value to the class, and sets the pointer to null. The destructor deletes the string memory.

Note that if you wanted to use this class in a broader scope, to include assignments of objects of the class to one another, you would need to build an overloaded assignment operator like the one in Exercise 7.18.

A member function named **PrevEntry** returns the pointer to the previous entry in the list. Another member function displays the current entry.

The member function of concern here is named **AddEntry**. It builds the list by putting the address of the current entry into the pointer of the next entry. It does this by copying the **this** pointer into the **preventry** pointer of the argument entry.

The main function of the program prompts you to enter some names at the console. After the last name you should enter the word **end**. Then the function navigates the list and displays the entries. Because the list pointers point from the current to the previous entry, the names display in the opposite order in which you entered them.

Note the use of the **new** operator to allocate memory for the **ListEntry** object to which the list pointer points. Chapter 3 addresses **new** and **delete** but does not discuss those operators with respect to classes because you had not learned about classes. A later section in this chapter discusses the free store as it pertains to objects of classes.

Arrays of Class Objects

A class object is just like any other C++ data type in that you can declare pointers to them and arrays of them. The array notation is the same as that of an array of structures.

Exercise 7.21 shows an array of **Date** structures.

```
#include <iostream.h>

// ------- date class
class Date {
    int mo, da, yr;
public:
    Date() { mo = 0; da = 0; yr = 0; }
    Date(int m, int d, int y) { mo = m; da = d; yr = y;}
    void display()
        { cout << '\n' << mo << '/' << da << '/' <<yr; }
};
main()
{
    Date dates[2];
    Date temp(6,24,40);

    dates[0] = temp;
    dates[0].display();
    dates[1].display();
}
```

Exercise 7.21 Arrays of Classes.

The constructor function in Exercise 7.21 for declarations without initializers initializes the three data members to zero. The main function declares an array of two **Dates** and a single date with initialized values. It assigns the initialized **Date** to the first of the two **Dates** in the array and then displays both dates as follows:

```
6/24/40
0/0/0
```

Class Array Constructors

When you declare an array of objects of a class, the compiler calls the constructor function once for each element in the array. It is important that you understand this relationship when you design constructor functions.

Exercise 7.22 repeats Exercise 7.21, but it adds a display message to the constructor function to prove that the constructor gets called twice for one declaration.

```
#include <iostream.h>

// ------- date class
class Date {
    int mo, da, yr;
public:
    Date();
    Date(int m, int d, int y) { mo = m; da = d; yr = y;}
    void display()
        { cout << '\n' << mo << '/' << da << '/' <<yr; }
};

// constructor that is called for each element in a Date array
Date::Date()
{
    cout << "\nDate constructor running";
    mo = 0; da = 0; yr = 0;
}

main()
{
    Date dates[2];
    Date temp(6,24,40);
```

Exercise 7.22 Constructors for Arrays of Classes.

```
    dates[0] = temp;
    dates[0].display();
    dates[1].display();
}
```

Exercise 7.22 Constructors for Arrays of Classes (continued).

Exercise 7.22 displays the following messages:

```
Date constructor running
Date constructor running
6/24/40
0/0/0
```

As you can see, the constructor function executed twice, once for each of the elements in the array. There is no message displayed for the constructor of the **temp** object because it uses the constructor function that accepts initializers, which has no message.

Class Array Destructors

When an array of objects of a class goes out of scope, the compiler calls the destructor function once for each element of the array.

Exercise 7.23 illustrates calling destructors for class-array elements.

```
#include <iostream.h>

// ------- date class
class Date {
    int mo, da, yr;
public:
    Date() { mo = 0; da = 0; yr = 0; }
    Date(int m, int d, int y) { mo = m; da = d; yr = y;}
    ~Date();
    void display()
        { cout << '\n' << mo << '/' << da << '/' <<yr; }
};

// destructor that is called for each element in a Date array
Date::~Date()
{
    cout << "\nDate destructor running";
}

main()
{
    Date dates[2];
    Date temp(6,24,40);

    dates[0] = temp;
    dates[0].display();
    dates[1].display();
}
```

Exercise 7.23 Destructors for Arrays of Classes (continued).

This exercise copies Exercise 7.22, except that there is a destructor function, which does nothing except display its execution on the console to prove that it runs more than once for an array of objects. The following display shows that the destructor runs three times—twice for the two elements in the dates array and once for the temp object:

```
6/24/40
0/0/0
Date destructor running
Date destructor running
Date destructor running
```

Static Members

You can declare that a member of a class is *static*, in which case one and only one instance of it exists. It is accessible to all of the member functions. No instance of the class needs to be declared for the static members to exist, although unless a static member is public, it cannot be seen by the rest of the program.

The declaration of a static member in a class does not automatically define the variable, however. You must define it outside of the class definition for it to exist.

Static Data Members

You would use a static data member to maintain a global value that applies to all instances of the class. Member functions can modify this value, and all other objects of the class then see the modified value. As an example, consider the simple linked list that Exercise 7.20 used. The class merely defined the list entries. It was up to the using program to keep track of the end of the list.

Exercise 7.24 improves the linked-list example in Exercise 7.20 with a static data member that holds the address of the last entry in the list.

```
#include <iostream.h>
#include <string.h>

class ListEntry {
    static ListEntry *lastentry; // static list head pointer
    char *listvalue;
    ListEntry *nextentry;
public:
    ListEntry();
    ListEntry(char *);
    ~ListEntry() { delete listvalue;}
    ListEntry *NextEntry() { return nextentry; };
    void display() { cout << '\n' << listvalue; }
};

ListEntry *ListEntry::lastentry;

ListEntry::ListEntry()
{
    listvalue = 0;
    nextentry = 0;
    lastentry = this;
}

ListEntry::ListEntry(char *s)
{
    lastentry->nextentry = this;
    lastentry = this;
    listvalue = new char[strlen(s)+1];
    strcpy(listvalue, s);
```

Exercise 7.22 Constructors for Arrays of Classes.

```
        nextentry = 0;
    }

main()
{
    ListEntry listhead;    // ---- this is the list head
    // ---------- read in some names
    while (1)    {
        cout << "\nEnter a name ('end' when done): ";
        char name[25];
        cin >> name;
        if (strncmp(name, "end", 3) == 0)
            break;
        // -------- make a list entry of the name
        new ListEntry(name);
    }
    ListEntry *next = listhead.NextEntry();
    // ------- display the names
    while (next != 0)    {
        next->display();
        ListEntry *hold = next;
        next = next->NextEntry();
        // -------- delete the ListEntry
        delete hold;
    }
}
```

Exercise 7.24 Static Members and the Linked List (continued).

Exercise 7.24 displays the following prompting messages. Enter names until you are done, then enter "end." The program displays the names in the order in which you entered them.

```
Enter a name ('end' when done): Fred
Enter a name ('end' when done): Joe
Enter a name ('end' when done): Al
Enter a name ('end' when done): Walter
Enter a name ('end' when done): Julian
Enter a name ('end' when done): end

Fred

Joe

Al

Walter

Julian
```

This exercise represents a much-improved linked-list class. By using a static data member to keep a record of the end of the list, the class assumes all of the responsibility for list integrity. To use it, you must declare a class object with no initializers. The constructor for that form sets up a new list with a list entry as the list head. This constructor also initializes the static **lastentry** pointer to point to the list head entry. The **nextentry** pointer in that entry is initially null, but eventually it points to the first list entry that the program declares. That entry points to the one following it, and subsequent entries point to the ones following them. The last entry in the list always has a null value in its **nextentry** pointer.

The constructor function for a list entry adds the entry to the list, so there is no need for the **AddEntry** function of Exercise 7.20. Observe that Exercise 7.24 uses the **new** operator to declare a new entry, and that it does not assign the address returned by the **new** operator to a pointer. Because the constructor function records the address of the entry in the **nextentry** pointer of the previous entry, the program does not need to otherwise remember the address.

Finally, the linked-list class defined in Exercise 7.24 allows the program to retrieve the entries in the same order in which they were added. After you enter all of the names and type in the **end** input, the program displays those names in their original order, rather than in reverse order as did earlier versions of this program.

Static Member Functions

Member functions can be static as well. You can use static member functions to perform tasks in the name of the class or an object where the function does not need access to the members of any particular instance of the class. Usually you use a static member function when you need to access only the static data members of a class.

Static member functions have no **this** pointer. Inasmuch as they have no access to the nonstatic members, they cannot use the **this** pointer to point to anything.

Exercise 7.25 adds a static member function to the **ListEntry** class. In this exercise, the function displays the last entry in the list, which is always the entry you just keyed in.

```
#include <iostream.h>
#include <string.h>

class ListEntry {
    static ListEntry *lastentry; // a static list head pointer
    char *listvalue;
    ListEntry *nextentry;
public:
    ListEntry();
    ListEntry(char *);
    ~ListEntry() { delete listvalue; }
    ListEntry *NextEntry() { return nextentry; };
    void display() { cout << '\n' << listvalue; }
    // ------- a static member function
    static void showlast();
};

ListEntry *ListEntry::lastentry;
```

Exercise 7.25 Static Member Functions.

```
ListEntry::ListEntry()
{
    listvalue = 0;
    nextentry = 0;
    lastentry = this;
}
ListEntry::ListEntry(char *s)
{
    lastentry->nextentry = this;
    lastentry = this;
    listvalue = new char[strlen(s)+1];
    strcpy(listvalue, s);
    nextentry = 0;
}


// ---------- a static member function
void ListEntry::showlast()
{
    lastentry->display();
    cout << " is the last entry in the list";
}
main()
{
    ListEntry listhead;    // ---- this is the list head
    // ---------- read in some names
    while (1)    {
        cout << "\nEnter a name ('end' when done): ";
        char name[25];
        cin >> name;
```

Exercise 7.25 Static Member Functions (continued).

```
                if (strncmp(name, "end", 3) == 0)
                    break;
                // -------- make a list entry of the name
                new ListEntry(name);
                // ----- call the static member function
                ListEntry::showlast();
            }
            // ------- delete the entries
            ListEntry *next = listhead.NextEntry();
            while (next != 0)     {
                ListEntry *hold = next;
                next = next->NextEntry();
                // -------- delete the ListEntry
                delete hold;
            }
        }
```

Exercise 7.25 Static Member Functions (continued).

Exercise 7.25 displays the following prompting messages. Enter names until you are done, then enter **end**. The program builds a linked list as you go and displays the last name in the list each time you enter a new one.

```
Enter a name ('end' when done): Alan
Alan is the last entry in the list
Enter a name ('end' when done): Sharon
Sharon is the last entry in the list
Enter a name ('end' when done): Wendy
Wendy is the last entry in the list
Enter a name ('end' when done): Tyler
Tyler is the last entry in the list
Enter a name ('end' when done): end
```

The **showlast** function is static. As such, it cannot read or write the member functions of the object for which it is called. But, because it needs to use the static **lastentry** pointer and nothing else, the function can be static, too.

Static Public Members

If a static member is public, it is accessible to the entire program and is not bound to a particular object. You can call a public static member function from anywhere without associating it with a particular instance of the class. The program in Exercise 7.25 called the **showlast** static member function in the name of the **listhead** object. In fact, the use of the object was for notational purposes only. Because the function is static, it could have been called in the name of any object. Further, because it is public, it can be called without an object reference at all. A public static member function is not global. It exists only within the scope of the class in which it is defined. You can, however, call it from anywhere by prefixing it with the class name and using the **::** scope resolution operator.

Exercise 7.26 modifies Exercise 7.25 to demonstrate how to call a public static member function without associating it with a particular object of the class.

```cpp
#include <iostream.h>
#include <string.h>

class ListEntry {
    static ListEntry *lastentry; // a static list head pointer
    char *listvalue;
    ListEntry *nextentry;
public:
    ListEntry();
    ListEntry(char *);
    ~ListEntry() { delete listvalue; }
    ListEntry *NextEntry() { return nextentry; };
    void display() { cout << '\n' << listvalue; }
```

Exercise 7.26 Public Static Member Functions.

```
    // ------- a static member function
    static void showlast();
};

ListEntry *ListEntry::lastentry;

ListEntry::ListEntry()
{
    listvalue = 0;
    nextentry = 0;
    lastentry = this;
}
ListEntry::ListEntry(char *s)
{
    lastentry->nextentry = this;
    lastentry = this;
    listvalue = new char[strlen(s)+1];
    strcpy(listvalue, s);
    nextentry = 0;
}
// ---------- a static member function
void ListEntry::showlast()
{
    lastentry->display();
    cout << " is the last entry in the list";
}

main()
{
    ListEntry listhead;     // ---- this is the list head
```

Exercise 7.26 Public Static Member Functions (continued).

```
    // ---------- read in some names
    while (1)    {
        cout << "\nEnter a name ('end' when done): ";
        char name[25];
        cin >> name;
        if (strncmp(name, "end", 3) == 0)
            break;
        // -------- make a list entry of the name
        new ListEntry(name);
        // ----- call the static member function
        // ----- with no object reference
        ListEntry::showlast();
    }
    // ------- delete the entries
    ListEntry *next = listhead.NextEntry();
    while (next != 0)    {
        ListEntry *hold = next;
        next = next->NextEntry();
        // -------- delete the ListEntry
        delete hold;
    }
}
```

Exercise 7.26 Public Static Member Functions (continued).

Exercise 7.26 has the same displays and inputs as Exercise 7.25.

Public static members may be used when there is no instance of the class. Because they are both public and static and you can call them in the name of the class alone, you can use one before you declare an object of the class.

Exercise 7.27 illustrates a class with a public static data member that the program initializes before declaring any objects of the class.

```
#include <iostream.h>

class Date {
    int mo, da, yr;
public:
    static int format;      // 1 - mm/dd/yy, 2 - dd/mm/yy
    Date(int m , int d, int y) { mo - m; da - d; yr - y; }
    void display();
};

int Date::format;

void Date::display()
{
    if (format -- 1)
        cout << mo << '/' << da;
    else
        cout << da << '/' << mo;
    cout << '/' << yr;
}
main()
{
    char ch - '0';
    while (ch !- '3')     {
        cout << "\n  1 - mm/dd/yy";
        cout << "\n  2 - dd/mm/yy";
        cout << "\n  3 - quit\n   ";
        cin >> ch;
        if (ch -- '1' || ch -- '2')     {
```

Exercise 7.27 Using Public Static Members Without Objects.

```
              Date::format - ch - '0'; // no Date declared yet
              // ---- declare and display a date
              Date dt(6, 24, 40);
              dt.display();
         }
     }
 }
```

Exercise 7.27 Using Public Static Members Without Objects (continued).

The **Date** class has a public static data member named **format**, which controls whether the **display** member function displays the date in either the **mm/dd/yy** or the **dd/mm/yy** format. The program displays the following menu:

```
1 - mm/dd/yy
2 - dd/mm/yy
3 - quit
```

When you enter a **1** or a **2**, the program initializes the **format** data member for the **Date** class even though no **Date** objects are in scope. Then, the program declares and displays the **dt** variable. One of the following two displays occurs, depending on what you typed into the menu.

```
6/24/40
24/6/40
```

Classes and the Free Store

In Chapter 3, you learned about the C++ free store and the **new** and **delete** memory-management operators. This section discusses those operators and their special relationship to class definitions.

Using *new* and *delete* to Manage Object Scope

An automatic class object usually comes into scope when it is declared and goes out of scope when the program exits the block in which the object is declared. You can override this behavior by using the **new** operator to construct an object. The object exists until you use the **delete** operator to destroy it. To use this feature, you must remember the address returned by **new** so that you can send it to **delete**. You must also remember the type of object that the pointer points to, because **delete** must know what type of object you are deleting. The type of object to be deleted is a function of the type of the pointer that you send to the **delete** operator.

Constructors and *new,* Destructors and *delete*

You used **new** and **delete** in earlier exercises to get and release memory for classes. When you use **new** to get memory for a class, the **new** operator function calls the class's constructor function. When you use **delete** to return the memory, the **delete** operator function calls the class's destructor function.

Exercise 7.28 illustrates the relationships between **new** and the constructor functions and **delete** and the destructor function.

```
#include <iostream.h>

class Date    {
    int mo, da, yr;
public:
    Date();
    ~Date();
};


Date::Date()
{
    cout << "\nDate constructor";
}
```

Exercise 7.28 ***new*** *= Constructor,* ***delete*** *= Destructor.*

```
Date::~Date()
{
    cout << "\nDate destructor";
}

main()
{
    Date *dt = new Date;
    cout << "\nProcess the date";
    delete dt;
}
```

*Exercise 7.28 **new** = Constructor, **delete** = Destructor.*

The exercise defines a **Date** class with a constructor and destructor. These functions simply display messages that say they are running. When the **new** operator initializes the **dt** pointer, the constructor function executes. When the **delete** operator deletes the memory pointed to by the pointer, it calls the destructor function.

Exercise 7.28 displays the following messages:

```
Date constructor
Process the date
Date destructor
```

The Free Store and Class Arrays

You learned earlier that constructor and destructor functions are called once for every element in an array of class objects.

Exercise 7.29 illustrates an incorrect way to delete arrays of new classes.

```
#include <iostream.h>

class Date     {
    int mo, da, yr;
public:
    Date()  { cout << "\nDate constructor"; }
    ~Date() { cout << "\nDate destructor";  }
};

main()
{
    Date *dt = new Date[5];
    cout << "\nProcess the dates";
    delete dt;                  // Not enough deletes!
}
```

*Exercise 7.29 Deleting Arrays of **new** Classes.*

The **dt** pointer points to an array of five dates. The **Date** constructor function executes five times from the **new** operator because that is what the array notation tells the compiler to do. But the compiler has no indication from the call to **delete** that the pointer points to more than one **Date** object, so it builds only one call to the destructor function.

Exercise 7.29 displays the following messages:

```
Date constructor
Date constructor
Date constructor
Date constructor
Date constructor
Process the dates
Date destructor
```

To solve this problem, C++ allows you to tell the **delete** operator that the pointer being deleted points to an array. You do so by adding the **[ ]** subscript operator to the delete operator like this:

```
delete [] pointername;
```

Because of the way the **delete** operator works with arrays, programmers must be even more cautious about overloading the global **new** and **delete** operators in the manner described in Chapter 3. The **new** operator needs to remember the size and the number of elements in any array for which it provides memory so that the **delete** operator knows how many destructors to call and the array offsets to the address of the objects being destroyed.

Exercise 7.30 illustrates the correct use of the **delete** operator where an array is involved.

```
#include <iostream.h>

class Date    {
    int mo, da, yr;
public:
    Date()  { cout << "\nDate constructor"; }
    ~Date() { cout << "\nDate destructor";  }
};

main()
{
    Date *dt = new Date[5];
    cout << "\nProcess the dates";
    delete [] dt;                  // deleting 5 items
}
```

*Exercise 7.30 Correctly Deleting Arrays of **new** Classes.*

Exercise 7.30 displays the following messages:

```
Date constructor
Date constructor
Date constructor
Date constructor
Date constructor
Process the dates
Date destructor
Date destructor
Date destructor
Date destructor
Date destructor
```

Overloaded Class *new* and *delete*

Chapter 3 taught you how to manage memory by writing overloaded **new** and **delete** operator functions. Those overloaded operators were for global uses of **new** and **delete**. You can also overload **new** and **delete** from within the scope of a class definition. This feature allows a class to have its own custom **new** and **delete** operators. You usually use this feature to gain some performance benefit from class-specific knowledge about the memory requirements of a class that can avoid the general-purpose overhead of the global **new** and **delete** operators.

Suppose that you know that there are never more than a certain small number of instances of a class at any one time. You can allocate the necessary memory for all instances of that class and use class-specific **new** and **delete** operators to manage the memory.

Exercise 7.31 illustrates a class with overloaded **new** and **delete** operators that are specific to the class.

```
#include <iostream.h>
#include <string.h>
#include <stddef.h>

const int MAXNAMES = 5;

class Names    {
    char name[25];
public:
    void setname(char *s) { strcpy(name, s); }
    void display() { cout << '\n' << name; }
    void *operator new(size_t);
    void operator delete(void *);
};

// -------- simple memory pool to handle fixed number of Names
char pool[MAXNAMES] [sizeof(Names)];
int inuse[MAXNAMES];

// -------- overloaded new operator for the Names class
void *Names::operator new(size_t)
{
    for (int p = 0; p < MAXNAMES; p++)
        if (!inuse[p])    {
            inuse[p] = 1;
            return pool+p;
        }
    return 0;
}
```

*Exercise 7.31 Class-specific **new** and **delete** Operators.*

```
// --------- overloaded delete operator for the Names class
void Names::operator delete(void *p)
{
    inuse[((char *)p - pool[0]) / sizeof(Names)] = 0;
}
main()
{
    Names *nm[MAXNAMES];
    for (int i = 0; i < MAXNAMES; i++)    {
        cout << "\nEnter name # " << i+1 << ": ";
        char name[25];
        cin >> name;
        nm[i] = new Names;
        nm[i]->setname(name);
    }
    for (i = 0; i < MAXNAMES; i++)    {
        nm[i]->display();
        delete nm[i];
    }
}
```

*Exercise 7.31 Class-specific **new** and **delete** Operators (continued).*

Exercise 7.31 prompts you for five names and then displays them as shown here:

```
Enter name # 1: Harpo
Enter name # 2: Chico
Enter name # 3: Groucho
Enter name # 4: Zeppo
Enter name # 5: Karl
```

```
Harpo

Chico

Groucho

Zeppo

Karl
```

A class of **Names** is defined in Exercise 7.31. The class has a member function that lets a user of the class set the name value of an object of the class. It also has a member function to display the name. Then it defines its own **new** and **delete** operators. Because the program is guaranteed never to exceed MAX-NAMES names at one time, the programmer has decided to speed execution by overriding the default **new** and **delete** operators.

The simple memory pool that supports names is a **pool** character array with enough space to hold all of the concurrent **Names** the program expects. The associated **inuse** integer array contains a true/false integer for each **Name** to indicate if an entry in the **pool** is in use.

The overloaded **new** operator finds an unused entry in the **pool** and returns its address. The overloaded **delete** operator marks the specified entry as unused.

Although a class design includes overloaded **new** and **delete** operators, the overloaded operator functions are not called for allocations of arrays of objects of the class. Suppose that the program in Exercise 7.31 included these statements:

```
Names *nms = new Names[10];
// ...
delete [] nms;
```

These statements would call the global **new** and **delete** operators rather than the overloaded ones.

Overloaded **new** and **delete** functions within a class definition are always **static** and have no **this** pointer associated with the object being created or deleted. This is because the compiler calls the **new** function before it calls the class's constructor function, and it calls the **delete** function after it calls the destructor.

Exercise 7.32 demonstrates the sequence in which the constructor, destructor, and overloaded **new** and **delete** operator functions execute.

```
#include <iostream.h>

class Name    {
    char name[25];
public:
    Name()  { cout << "\nName constructor running"; }
    ~Name() { cout << "\nName destructor running";    }
    void *operator new(size_t);
    void operator delete(void *);
};

// -------- simple memory pool to handle one Name
char pool [sizeof(Name)];

// -------- overloaded new operator for the Name class
void *Name::operator new(size_t)
{
    cout << "\nName's new running";
    return pool;
}

// --------- overloaded delete operator for the Name class
void Name::operator delete(void *)
{
    cout << "\nName's delete running";
}

main()
{
    cout << "\nBuilding a new name";
```

*Exercise 7.32 Class-specific **new** and **delete** Operators with Constructor, Destructor.*

```
    Name *nm = new Name;
    cout << "\nDeleting a name";
    delete nm;
}
```

*Exercise 7.32 Class-specific **new** and **delete** Operators with Constructor, Destructor (continued).*

Exercise 7.32 does nothing with the class except display the following messages as the various functions execute.

```
Building a new name
Name's new running
Name constructor running
Deleting a name
Name destructor running
Name's delete running
```

As you can see, the **new** function executes before the constructor function. The **new** function may not access any of the class's members because no memory exists for them until **new** allocates it and because the constructor function has not yet performed any other class-specific initializations. Likewise, because the **delete** operator executes after the destructor function, the **delete** operator may not have access to the class members.

Copy Constructors

A *copy constructor* is a class member function that executes when you initialize a new object of the class with an existing object of the same class. The copy constructor is similar to the conversion constructor function that you learned about earlier in this chapter. Conversion constructors convert the values in one class object to the format of an object of a different type. Copy constructors initialize the values from an existing object of a class to a new instantiated object of that same class.

Earlier in this chapter you learned how to overload the assignment operator (=) to manage the assignment of an object of a class to another object of the same class where the default bit-wise assignment provided by the compiler would cause problems. Similar problems occur when you initialize an object with the contents of another object, so you must have copy constructor functions.

The difference between initialization of an object with another object and assignment of one object to another is this: assignment assigns the value of an existing object to another existing object; initialization creates a new object and initializes it with the contents of the existing object. The compiler can distinguish the two by using your overloaded assignment operator for assignments and your copy constructor for initializers. If you omit either one, the compiler builds a default member-by-member copy operation for the one you omit.

Initializing an object with the contents of another object of the same class requires the use of a copy constructor function, which is a constructor that can be called with a single argument of the same class as the object being constructed.

Exercise 7.33 demonstrates the copy constructor.

```
#include <iostream.h>
#include <string.h>

// ------- date class
class Date {
    int mo, da, yr;
    char *month;
public:
    Date(int m, int d, int y);
    Date(Date&);  // copy constructor
    ~Date();
    void display();
};
```

Exercise 7.33 Copy Constructor.

```
// constructor that is called for an initialized Date
Date::Date(int m, int d, int y)
{
    static char *mos[] = {
        "January", "February", "March", "April", "May",
        "June", "July", "August", "September", "October",
        "November", "December"
    };
    mo = m; da = d; yr = y;
    month = new char[strlen(mos[m-1])+1];
    strcpy(month, mos[m-1]);
}
// ---------- Date copy constructor
Date::Date(Date& dt)
{
    mo = dt.mo;
    da = dt.da;
    yr = dt.yr;
    month = new char [strlen(dt.month)+1];
    strcpy(month, dt.month);
}

// Destructor for a Date
Date::~Date()
{
    delete month;
}
```

Exercise 7.33 Copy Constructor (continued).

```
// ----------- display member function
void Date::display()
{
    if (month != 0)
        cout << '\n' << month << ' ' << da << ", "
            << yr+1900;
}


main()
{
    // ------ first date
    Date birthday(6,24,40);
    birthday.display();
    // ------ second date
    Date newday = birthday;
    newday.display();
    // ------ third date
    Date lastday(birthday);
    lastday.display();
}
```

Exercise 7.33 Copy Constructor (continued).

The copy constructor in this exercise resembles the overloaded assignment operator in Exercise 7.18. The difference is that the copy constructor function executes when you declare a new **Date** object that is to be initialized with the contents of an existing **Date** object. The exercise shows that there are two ways to do this. One way uses the usual C++ variable initializer syntax as shown here.

```
Date newday = birthday;
```

The second way uses the constructor calling convention where the initializing object is an argument to the function's parameter as shown here:

```
Date lastday(birthday);
```

References in Classes

Chapter 6 taught you about references. Everything that you learned about using references with the standard C++ data types and structures applies equally to objects of classes. Using references to class objects as function parameters and return values adds a measure of efficiency that would not exist if you had to pass every object by value.

You can declare references as class data members as well, but there are some things to consider. First, remember that a reference must be initialized. You do not usually initialize a class object with a brace-surrounded initialization list like you do a structure. You initialize it with a constructor. Therefore, class member references must be initialized by the class constructor. Remember, too, that references are aliases. References in classes behave just as if they were data members of the class with the same notational syntax, but operations on member references actually operate on the objects that are used to initialize them. Exercise 7.34 shows the use of a class that has reference data members.

```
#include <iostream.h>

class Date  {
    int da, mo, yr;
public:
    Date(int d,int m,int y)
        { da = d; mo = m; yr = y; }
    void Display()
        { cout << da << '/' << mo << '/' << yr; }
};
```

Exercise 7.34 A Class with a Reference.

```
class Time  {
    int hr, min, sec;
public:
    Time(int h, int m, int s)
        { hr = h; min = m; sec = s; }
    void Display()
        { cout << hr << ':' << min << ':' << sec; }
};

class DateTime {
    Date& dt;        // reference to Date
    Time& tm;        // reference to Time
public:
    // --- constructor with reference initializers
    DateTime(Date& d, Time& t) : dt(d), tm(t)
        { /* empty */ }
    void Display()
        { dt.Display(); cout << ' '; tm.Display(); }
};

main()
{
    Date today(25,3,93);
    Time now(4,15,0);
    DateTime dtm(today, now);
    dtm.Display();
}
```

Exercise 7.34 A Class with a Reference (continued).

Observe the **DateTime** constructor specification. The **colon** operator specifies that a list of initializers follows. You must initialize references in this manner.

You cannot wait and do it in the body of the constructor. If the constructor is not **inline**, as this one is, you put the colon and list in the constructor's declaration rather than in its prototype in the class definition.

Exercise 7.34 displays the following:

```
25/3/93 4:15:0
```

The Management of Class Source and Object Files

In all of the previous exercises, each program has been a single, stand-alone source module. The entire program was contained in one source module that represented the exercise. In actual practice, you do not organize a C++ source program that way. You use the traditional C convention of having common definitions in header files, common executable code in separately compiled object libraries, and separately compiled source code files for the code that supports your application.

Class Definitions in a Header

The convention for C++ header files resembles that of C. Put things in header files that do not reserve memory but that define structures, classes, and externally defined items to the source modules that include header files. Where a class uses the definitions of other classes, its **include** file includes those of the other classes. This opens the possibility for multiple or circular inclusions. You should use a code convention that prevents the errors that could occur if a source file is included twice or if source file A includes source file B, which includes source file C, which includes source file A.

If you have a class named **Date**, for example, you might put its definition in a header file named **date.h**. If you use the **#ifndef** preprocessor directive shown in the following listing, you can prevent those cases where a header file might be included more than once or where header file inclusion wraps around.

```
#ifndef DATE_H
#define DATE_H
// --- the contents of date.h
#endif
```

Class Member Functions in a Library

As a general rule, you should separately compile the member functions of your classes and maintain them as separate object files, perhaps in object library files. The source files for the member functions will, of course, include the header files that define the classes to which the functions belong, as well as those for any classes that they may use and that might not be included from within the class header.

Summary

This chapter taught you about C++ classes. Chapter 8 is about overloaded operators, a feature touched on here and in Chapter 3. In Chapter 3, you learned to overload the **new** and **delete** operators to insert your own memory-management functions into the program. In this chapter you learned the same technique, but at the individual class level. You also learned to overload the assignment operator to build conversion functions and to manage class copying where a binary or member-by-member copy would not work.

The potential for overloaded operators extends beyond the uses you've learned so far. With them you can perform arithmetic, comparisons, and many other operations on your classes just as if they were standard C++ data types. Chapter 8 describes these features.

Chapter

8

Overloaded Operators

This chapter is about extending the C++ language by adding operators to classes. A C++ class effectively adds a new data type to the language. You learned how to add dates and other such types by binding data structures and functions. Now you will add to those classes the behavior of C++ operators. You will learn how to overload:

- Arithmetic operators
- Relational operators
- Assignment operators
- Auto increment and decrement operators
- Unary operators
- The subscript operator
- The function call operator
- The pointer-to-member operator
- An improved overloaded assignment operator

Consider a class to implement a numerical type. The using program must compute the sum of a column of objects of the type. It must also be able to increment, decrement, and add and subtract other numerical types to and from objects of the class. The program needs to compare two of the objects to see if they are equal or which is greater. You could build special class member functions to perform these operations and call them the way you call the standard C function **strcmp**, for example. There is, however, a better way.

C++ lets you build operators that implement unary and binary operations on objects of classes. This feature is called *operator overloading*, and with it you add member functions to the class to implement the overloaded operators.

In Chapters 3 and 7 you overloaded the **new** and **delete** operators to build custom memory management. In Chapter 7 you overloaded the assignment operator to build conversion and copy functions for your classes. You have already used overloaded operators extensively in most of the exercises. Every time you display a value on the **cout** object, you use the << bit-wise shift left operator, which is overloaded by the **ostream** class.

Overloading an operator means that you write a function to make the operator do your bidding. For example, you can do these operations with a **Date** class:

```
Date dt1(1,2,83);
Date dt2(2,4,93);
dt1 += 100;              // add 100 days
int dif = dt2-dt1;       // compute the delta
if (dt2 < dt1)           // compare two dates
    dt1 = dt2;           // assign dates
cout << dt1 << ' ' << dt2; // display the dates
```

Look at the last of the examples just shown. You will learn how to overload the << and >> operators in Chapter 10.

Overloaded operators must obey some some rules:

1. The overloaded operator must comply with the syntax of the language. For example, you cannot do the following in C++:

```
int a;
/ a;    // error: / is not a unary operator
```

Therefore, you cannot overload the / operator to do the following either:

```
Date dt(1,2,83);
/ dt;    // error: / is not a unary operator
```

2. If you can put an operator between two identifiers, then you can overload it for custom use with your classes, even if the operator would not be otherwise acceptable to the compiler. Consider the following statement:

```
cout << "Hello";
```

Without an overloaded << operator, that expression seems to shift **cout** a number of bits equal to the value of the pointer to the string, none of which would have passed the compiler's error check. But the statement is correct syntax, so you can write an overloaded operator function that executes when this construct appears. The compiler sees the overloaded operator in the context of the two data types and associates this statement with it.

3. You cannot overload the way an operator works with the intrinsic C++ data types. For example, you cannot overload the binary integer addition operator.

4. You cannot invent new operators that do not exist in the C++ language. For example, the dollar sign ($) is not a C++ operator, so it cannot be an overloaded operator.

5. You cannot overload these operators:

```
Operator    Definition
    .       Class member operator
   .*       Pointer-to-member operator
   ::       Scope resolution operator
   ?:       Conditional expression operator
```

6. You cannot change the precedence of operator evaluation.

Binary Arithmetic Operators

Consider a **Date** class like the ones in Chapter 7. You want to compute a new **Date** object by adding an integer number of days to an existing one. You could write a member function and call it as shown here:

```
newdate.AddToDate(100);
```

Rather than calling a function to make the addition, you prefer to use this more intuitive syntax:

```
newdate = newdate + 100;
```

Assuming that **newdate** is an object of type **Date** with a value already in it and that you have correctly overloaded the binary addition operator (+) in this context, the result would be the **newdate** object of type **Date** with the month, day, and year incremented by 100 days.

Class Member Operator Functions

To perform the kind of addition on objects of a class just shown, you write a class member function that overloads the binary addition (+) operator when it appears between a **Date** object and an integer.

Exercise 8.1 overloads an operator to compute the sum of an integer and an object of the **Date** class returning an object of the **Date** class.

```
#include <iostream.h>

class Date {
    int mo, da, yr;
public:
    Date(int m=0, int d=0, int y=0)
        { mo = m; da = d; yr = y; }
```

Exercise 8.1 Overloading the + Operator.

```
    void display()
        { cout << mo << '/' << da << '/' << yr; }
    Date operator+(int);        // overloaded + operator
};

static int dys[]={31,28,31,30,31,30,31,31,30,31,30,31};
// -------- overloaded + operator
Date Date::operator+(int n)
{
    Date dt = *this;
    n += dt.da;
    while (n > dys[dt.mo-1])    {
        n -= dys[dt.mo-1];
        if (++dt.mo == 13)    {
            dt.mo = 1;
            dt.yr++;
        }
    }
    dt.da = n;
    return dt;
}

main()
{
    Date olddate(2,20,90);
    Date newdate;
    newdate = olddate + 21;    // three weeks hence
    newdate.display();
}
```

Exercise 8.1 Overloading the + Operator (continued).

Exercise 8.1 displays the following date:

```
3/13/90
```

Here is how the overloaded operator function works. When the compiler sees the expression, **olddate + 21**, it recognizes that **olddate** is an object of type **Date** and that the **Date** class includes an overloaded binary addition operator function. The compiler substitutes a call to the overloaded operator function with the integer value as the argument. You could code the substituted call yourself this way:

```
newdate = olddate.operator+(21);
```

The **operator+** part of the statement is the name of the member function. The **21** is the integer argument to its only parameter. While you can call an overloaded operator function this way, they are meant to be used in the context of an expression that uses the operator as in:

```
newdate = olddate + 21;
```

Remember the discussion on the overloaded assignment operator in Chapter 7. If the **Date** class has an overloaded assignment operator function, the statement just shown will call it after calling the overloaded binary addition operator function to assign the result to **newdate**. Since Exercise 8.1 has no overloaded assignment operator, the compiler creates a default one to make a bit-for-bit copy of the original.

Observe that the overloaded binary addition operator function in Exercise 8.1 does not modify the **Date** object in the expression. The **olddate** object declared in the main function retains its value. This behavior mimics that of similar expressions with intrinsic numerical types. This is a valuable lesson. Strive to overload operators in intuitive ways.

Nonmember Operator Functions

Exercise 8.1 overloads the + operator by using a member function. Like other member functions, overloaded operator member functions are associated with the object for which the operator function executes. In this case, the object is the **olddate** object taken from the left side of the binary expression. But suppose you wanted to support the following expression as well:

```
Date newdate = 100 + olddate;
```

There is no way to design a class member overloaded operator function to support an expression like that. You can, however, write a nonmember **friend** function to overload the operator and get what you want.

Exercise 8.2 adds a **friend** function to the program in Exercise 8.1 to overload the binary addition (+) operator.

```cpp
#include <iostream.h>

class Date {
    int mo, da, yr;
public:
    Date(int m=0, int d=0, int y=0)
        { mo = m; da = d; yr = y; }
    void display()
        { cout << mo << '/' << da << '/' << yr; }
    // ----- overloaded + operators
    Date operator+(int);
    friend Date operator+(int n, Date& dt);
};

static int dys[]={31,28,31,30,31,30,31,31,30,31,30,31};
// -------- overloaded + operator: Date + int
Date Date::operator+(int n)
{
    Date dt = *this;
    n += dt.da;
```

*Exercise 8.2 Overloading the + Operator with a **Friend**.*

```
        while (n > dys[dt.mo-1])      {
            n -= dys[dt.mo-1];
            if (++dt.mo == 13)       {
                dt.mo = 1;
                dt.yr++;
            }
        }
        dt.da = n;
        return dt;
    }
    // ----- overloaded operator: int + Date
    Date operator+(int n, Date& dt)
    {
        return dt + n;
    }
    main()
    {
        Date olddate(2,20,90);
        Date newdate;
        newdate = 11 + olddate + 10;   // three weeks hence
        newdate.display();
    }
```

*Exercise 8.2 Overloading the + Operator with a **Friend** (continued).*

Exercise 8.2 displays the same output as Exercise 8.1.

The overloaded **friend** function uses the class's overloaded **operator+** function to perform the addition.

Overloaded operator functions such as the **friend** function in Exercise 8.2 have both parameters declared. The function is not a member of a class. Since it does not execute as a class member function, there is no implied object.

Incidentally, you could write the first overloaded binary addition function as a **friend** function as well. Some programmers overload all of their class operators as **friend** functions just for consistency.

Observe that the expression in the using program now uses two integer constants to compute the result. The effective expression is **(11+olddate)+10**. The first part uses the overloaded **friend** function and the second part uses the overloaded member function. With these two overloaded functions you can write an expression that consists of a **Date** object and any number of integer expressions and compute the effective new **Date** object. You would probably not add two dates because the result would not be meaningful. You could, however, use overloaded subtraction to compute the number of days between two dates.

A word of caution: Nothing says that an overloaded binary addition operator function must perform addition. For example, string classes often overload the plus operator to concatenate strings the way that **Basic** does. An overloaded operator function does whatever you design it to do. It causes the compiler to call the function when the operator is applied a context that matches the parameter types. Then the function does whatever you code it it to do. You might have guessed by now that you could overload the addition operator to perform subtraction. Yes, you could, but it is not a wise thing to do.

The examples just given deal with addition. You can use the same approaches to develop overloaded subtraction, multiplication, division, relational, modulus, Boolean, and shifting operator functions. Once again, nothing requires you to make those functions perform intuitively, and there are a lot of C++ programs with wildly overloaded operators that only their creators can understand. If you must overload operators, always try to overload them so that they perform operations that resemble their use with intrinsic data types in the C++ language.

Relational Operators

Suppose you want to compare dates. Perhaps you need to use an expression such as the following one:

```
if (newdate < olddate)
    // ....
```

You can overload relational operators the same way that you overloaded the addition operator.

Exercise 8.3 shows the **Date** class with overloaded operators that compare dates.

```
#include <iostream.h>

class Date {
    int mo, da, yr;
public:
    Date(int m=0, int d=0, int y=0)
        { mo = m; da = d; yr = y; }
    void display()
        { cout << mo << '/' << da << '/' << yr; }
    // ----- overloaded operators
    int operator==(Date& dt);
    int operator<(Date&);
};
// ----- overloaded equality operator
int Date::operator==(Date& dt)
{
    return (this->mo == dt.mo &&
            this->da == dt.da &&
            this->yr == dt.yr);
}
// ----- overloaded less than operator
int Date::operator<(Date& dt)
{
    if (this->yr == dt.yr)    {
        if (this->mo == dt.mo)
```

Exercise 8.3 Overloading Relational Operators.

```
                return this->da < dt.da;
            return this->mo < dt.mo;
        }
        return this->yr < dt.yr;
    }
main()
{
    Date date1(12,7,41),
         date2(2,22,90),
         date3(12,7,41);

    if (date1 < date2)    {
        date1.display();
        cout << " is less than ";
        date2.display();
    }
    cout << '\n';
    if (date1 == date3)    {
        date1.display();
        cout << " is equal to ";
        date3.display();
    }
}
```

Exercise 8.3 Overloading Relational Operators (continued).

The **Date** class in Exercise 8.3 has two overloaded relational operators, the equal to (==) and the less than (<) operators. The main function declares three dates, compares them, and displays the following messages:

```
12/7/41 is less than 2/22/90
12/7/41 is equal to 12/7/41
```

You could easily build the other relational operators as variations on the two that the exercise has. For example, the != (not equal) operator could be coded the following way:

```
int operator!=(Date& dt) { return !(*this == dt); }
```

More Assignment Operators

You already learned how to overload the assignment operator (=) in the discussion on conversion and assignment functions in Chapter 7. C++ has other assignment operators (+=, -=, <<=, >>=, |=, &=, ^=) where the assignment includes an arithmetic, Boolean, or shift operation applied to the receiving field. You can overload these operators to work with your classes.

Exercise 8.4 adds the overloaded += operator to the **Date** class by using the overloaded + operator that the class already has.

```
#include <iostream.h>

class Date {
    int mo, da, yr;
public:
    Date(int m=0, int d=0, int y=0)
        { mo = m; da = d; yr = y; }
    void display()
        { cout << mo << '/' << da << '/' << yr; }
    // --------- overloaded + operator
    Date operator+(int);
    // --------- overloaded += operator
    Date operator+=(int n)
```

Exercise 8.4 Overloading the += Operator.

```
             { *this = *this + n; return *this; }
};

static int dys[]={31,28,31,30,31,30,31,31,30,31,30,31};
// -------- overloaded + operator
Date Date::operator+(int n)
{
    Date dt = *this;
    n += dt.da;
    while (n > dys[dt.mo-1])     {
        n -= dys[dt.mo-1];
        if (++dt.mo == 13)     {
            dt.mo = 1;
            dt.yr++;
        }
    }
    dt.da = n;
    return dt;
}

main()
{
    Date olddate(2,20,90);
    olddate += 21;             // three weeks hence
    olddate.display();
}
```

Exercise 8.4 Overloading the += Operator (continued).

Exercise 8.4 displays the same output as Exercises 8.1 and 8.2.

Auto-increment and Auto-decrement

You can overload the auto-increment (++) and the auto-decrement (--) operators and specify whether these operators are prefix or postfix.

```
Date dt;
++dt;   // calls the overloaded prefix ++ operator
dt++;   // calls the overloaded postfix ++ operator
```

Exercise 8.5 adds the overloaded auto-increment (++) prefix and postfix operators to the **Date** class by using the overloaded binary addition operator that the class already has.

```cpp
#include <iostream.h>

class Date {
    int mo, da, yr;
public:
    Date(int m=0, int d=0, int y=0)
        { mo = m; da = d; yr = y; }
    void display()
        { cout << '\n' << mo << '/' << da << '/' << yr;}
    Date operator+(int);        // overloaded +
    // --------- overloaded prefix ++ operator
    Date operator++()
        { *this = *this + 1; return *this; }
    // --------- overloaded postfix ++ operator
    Date operator++(int)
        { Date dt=*this; *this=*this+1; return dt; }
};
```

Exercise 8.5 Overloading the ++ Operator.

```
static int dys[]={31,28,31,30,31,30,31,31,30,31,30,31};
// -------- overloaded + operator
Date Date::operator+(int n)
{
    Date dt = *this;
    n += dt.da;
    while (n > dys[dt.mo-1])     {
        n -= dys[dt.mo-1];
        if (++dt.mo == 13)     {
            dt.mo = 1;
            dt.yr++;
        }
    }
    dt.da = n;
    return dt;
}

main()
{
    Date olddate(2,20,90);
    olddate++;
    olddate.display();
    ++olddate;
    olddate.display();
}
```

Exercise 8.5 Overloading the ++ Operator (continued).

Exercise 8.5 displays these dates.

```
2/21/90
2/22/90
```

As shown in the exercise, you can specify that the auto-increment and auto-decrement operators are prefix or postfix as shown here.

```
Date operator++();      // prefix ++ operator
Date operator++(int);   // postfix ++ operator
```

The compiler will call the overloaded prefix operator function when it sees the prefix notation. The unnamed **int** variable in the overloaded postfix operator function declaration tells the compiler to call this function for the postfix operator. Note that the compiler makes no further distinction other than to call the correct function. The code in the functions is responsible for supporting prefix or postfix operations. In Exercise 8.5, the overloaded **operator++()** function increments the object and returns it. The overloaded **operator++(int)** function saves the value of the object before incrementing it and then returns the saved object.

Address-of and Reference-to Operator

You can overload the unary address-of **(&)** operator to change its behavior. One possible use for the overloaded **&** operator is to take the address of one of the data members, usually the most significant one, to pass to a library function that expects an address. Exercise 8.6 overloads the **&** operator to return the address of a data member.

```
#include <iostream.h>
#include <string.h>

class Name {
    char name[25];
public:
    void display()
        { cout << '\n' << name; }
    // ---- add a name
```

Exercise 8.6 Overloaded & Operator.

```
      void AddName(char *nm)
          { strncpy(name, nm, 24); name[24] = '\0'; }
      // ---- overloaded & address-of operator
      const char * operator&()
          { return name; }
};

main()
{
    char nm[25];
    Name names[5];
    for (int i = 0; i < 5; i++)     {
        cout << "\nEnter a name: ";
        cin >> nm;
        names[i].AddName(nm);
    }
    for (i = 0; i < 5; i++)
        cout << '\n' << &names[i];
}
```

Exercise 8.6 Overloaded & Operator (continued).

In Exercise 8.6, you enter five names in response to the prompt. The program then displays the names in the order in which you entered them:

```
Enter a name: John
Enter a name: Bill
Enter a name: Terry
Enter a name: Warren
Enter a name: Lou
```

```
John
Bill
Terry
Warren
Lou
```

The exercise overloads the **&** operator to return the address of the **name** array from within the class. The operator returns a **const** character pointer, which means that users of the function may not use the address to modify the data values in the object. The address may be used only in contexts where a **const** character pointer is expected. The input from **cin** may not, therefore, go to that address. The class uses the **AddName** member function to change an object's data value.

Conversely, the output to **cout** may go to the address that the overloaded operator function returns because that context expects a const pointer and does not intend to modify the data.

 If you overload the **&** operator with a class for any purpose, you can no longer use the operator to take the address of an object of the class. Rather than overloading **&**, you should use a member function to return the address of the data member of an object and let the **&** operator perform its normal function.

Unary Plus and Minus Operators

You can overload the unary plus and minus operators to work with a class. Suppose you have a class that describes an inventory quantity and you need to express that quantity with the plus and minus unary operators. Exercise 8.7 is an example of how overloading the unary minus operator might work.

```
#include <iostream.h>
#include <string.h>

class ItemQty {
    int onhand;
    char desc[25];
public:
    ItemQty(int oh, char *d)
        { onhand = oh; strcpy(desc, d); }
    void display()
        { cout << '\n' << desc << ": " << onhand; }
    // ---- overloaded unary - operator
    int operator-() { return -onhand; }
};

main()
{
    ItemQty item1(100, "crankshaft");
    ItemQty item2(-50, "driveshaft");
    item1.display();
    cout << '\n' << -item1;  // invoke the overloaded -
    item2.display();
    cout << '\n' << -item2;  // invoke the overloaded -
}
```

Exercise 8.7 Overloaded Unary Minus.

The exercise declares two **ItemQty** objects, one with a positive **onhand** value and one with a negative. It calls the **display** function to display the record contents and then uses the overloaded unary minus operator to display the quantity with the unary minus operator applied, as shown in the following display:

```
crankshaft: 100
-100
driveshaft: -50
50
```

Subscript Operator

Overloading the subscript ([]) operator is sometimes worth doing. For example, a **String** class that stores a string value can overload the subscript operator to provide subscripted access to the character positions of the string value.

Exercise 8.8 overloads the [] operator in a small string class.

```
#include <iostream.h>
#include <string.h>

class String     {
    char *sptr;
public:
    String(char *s = 0);
    ~String() { delete sptr; }
    void display()
        { cout << '\n' << sptr; }
    // --- overloaded [] operator
    char& operator[] (int n)
        { return *(sptr + n); }
};

String::String(char *s)
{
```

Exercise 8.8 Overloaded [ ] Operator.

```
    if (s)  {
        sptr = new char[strlen(s)+1];
        strcpy(sptr, s);
    }
    else
        sptr = 0;
}

main()
{
    String mystring("The Ides of March");
    mystring.display();
    cout << '\n' << mystring[4];
    mystring[4] = '1';
    mystring[5] = '5';
    mystring[6] = 't';
    mystring[7] = 'h';
    mystring.display();
    strncpy(&mystring[4], "21st", 4);
    mystring.display();
}
```

Exercise 8.8 Overloaded [ ] Operator (continued).

The exercise declares a string with a value. The overloaded [] operator function allows the program to retrieve a single character from the string. Because the [] operator function returns a reference to the character being subscripted, the program can use the expression on the left side of an assignment. With that notation, the program inserts the value "15th" one character at a time into the string and displays it. Then, by using the address of the value returned, the program uses **strncpy** to insert the value "21s" into the string and displays it.

Exercise 8.8 displays the following messages when you run it:

```
The Ides of March
I
The 15th of March
The 21st of March
```

Note that the overloaded [ ] subscript operator must be a nonstatic member function. You cannot implement it as a **friend** function like you can other operators.

Suppose you wanted to continue the similarity between your string classes and the character arrays of C++, where the following expressions are equivalent:

```
mystring[5]
*(mystring+5)
```

The following expressions are also equivalent:

```
&mystring[5]
mystring+5;
```

Exercise 8.9 shows how the overloaded + operator can simulate dereferenced pointer notation in a string class.

```cpp
#include <iostream.h>
#include <string.h>

class String    {
    char *sptr;
public:
    String(char *);
    ~String() { delete sptr; }
    void display()
        { cout << '\n' << sptr; }
    // --- overloaded [] operator
```

Exercise 8.9 Overloaded + Operator.

```
        char& operator[] (int n)
            { return *(sptr + n); }
        // --- overloaded () operator
        char *operator+ (int n)
            { return sptr + n; }
};

String::String(char *s)
{
    if (s) {
        sptr = new char[strlen(s)+1];
        strcpy(sptr, s);
    }
    else
        sptr = 0;
}

main()
{
    String mystring("The Ides of March");
    mystring.display();
    cout << '\n' << *(mystring+4);
    *(mystring+4) = '1';
    *(mystring+5) = '5';
    *(mystring+6) = 't';
    *(mystring+7) = 'h';
    mystring.display();
    strncpy(mystring+4, "21st", 4);
    mystring.display();
}
```

Exercise 8.9 Overloaded + Operator (continued).

The exercise adds the overloaded + operator and changes its annotation from subscripted array accesses of the string to dereferenced pointer accesses. Other than for those differences, Exercise 8.9 is the same as Exercise 8.8.

This particular usage would not prevent you from using the + operator as a Basic-like string concatenation operator as well. As shown here, you can overload an overloaded operator function by using different parameter types the same way you can for other functions:

```
class String {
    // ...
public:
    // ...
    char *operator+(int n);
    String& operator+(String& s);
};
```

The **String** class in these examples is not complete. Its purpose is to illustrate operator overloading and is not intended to be used as a rugged string class. The companion diskette includes a complete string class that you can study and use. Most compilers include their own versions of string classes. The C++ ANSI standardization procedure, when completed, will no doubt define a standard string class for the language.

Function Call Operator

Overloading the () function call operator makes your object's name look like a function that accepts whatever arguments you specify. How you use the overloaded () function call operator depends on your class and your imagination. Whether or not you really want to do it will depend on how far from traditional C++ styles you want to wander. As with all operator overloading, you should be reluctant to overload () where its purpose is not apparent.

Exercise 8.10 illustrates one possibility for using the overloaded () operator.

```
#include <iostream.h>
#include <string.h>

class Name {
    char name[25];
public:
    Name(char *s)
        { strcpy(name, s); }
    void operator() (char *s, int n)
        { strncpy(s, name, n); *(s+n) = '\0'; }
};

main()
{
    Name nm("Charlie");
    char newname[25];
    // --- use overloaded () to get name value
    nm(newname, sizeof newname -1);
    cout << newname;
}
```

Exercise 8.10 Overloaded () Operator.

Exercise 8.10 displays the name "Charlie" on the screen.

The exercise uses the overloaded () operator with a **char** pointer as an argument to deliver the contents of the **Name** class to the caller. You can use several different versions of the overloaded () operator as long as each one has a distinct parameter list.

Note that the overloaded () function call operator must be a nonstatic member function. You cannot implement it as a **friend** function in the manner of other operators.

Pointer-to-member Operator

The -> operator, when overloaded, is always a postfix unary operator with the class object (or reference to same) on its left. The overloaded operator function returns the address of an object of some class.

Although the overloaded -> operator is postfix unary, its use requires the name of a member on the right side of the expression. That member must be a member of the class for which the overloaded operator returns an address.

You can overload the -> operator to assure that a pointer to a class object always has a value, in other words to build, a smart pointer to an object. The pointer always guarantees that it points to something meaningful, and you avoid problems associated with de-referencing null and garbage pointers.

To illustrate the need for a smart pointer, Exercise 8.11 uses the usual **Date** class and, at the beginning of the program, a pointer to an object of the **Date** class.

```
#include <iostream.h>

class Date {
    int mo, da, yr;
public:
    Date(int m=0, int d=0, int y=0)
        { mo = m; da = d; yr = y; }
    void display()
        { cout << '\n' << mo << '/' << da << '/' << yr; }
};

main()
{
    Date *dp;            // date pointer with garbage in it
    Date dt(3,17,90);    // Date
    dp = &dt;            // put address of date in pointer
    dp->display();       // display date through the pointer
}
```

Exercise 8.11 Pointer to Class Object.

Exercise 8.11 displays the date 3/17/90 on the screen.

The program declares a **Date** object, puts its address in the pointer, and calls the **display** member function through the pointer. Nothing is wrong with that. However, if the programmer neglects to assign a valid address of a **Date** object to the pointer, the program crashes because the pointer points nowhere meaningful. Whatever gets executed by that function call is not likely to be a valid function.

Exercise 8.12 overloads the -> operator to adds a so-called smart pointer to the program.

```
#include <iostream.h>

class Date {
    int mo, da, yr;
public:
    Date(int m=0, int d=0, int y=0)
            { mo = m; da = d; yr = y; }
    void display()
        { cout << '\n' << mo << '/' << da << '/' << yr; }
};
// ---------- "smart" Date pointer
class DatePtr {
    Date *dp;
public:
    DatePtr(Date *d = 0) { dp = d; }
    Date *operator->();
};

Date *DatePtr::operator->()
{
    static Date nulldate(0,0,0);
```

Exercise 8.12 Overloaded -> Operator.

```
        if (dp == 0)            // if the pointer is NULL
            return &nulldate;   // return the dummy address
        return dp;              // otherwise return the pointer
    }


main()
{
    DatePtr dp;         // date pointer with nothing in it
    dp->display();      // use it to call display function
    Date dt(3,17,90);   // Date
    dp = &dt;           // put address of date in pointer
    dp->display();      // display date through the pointer
}
```

Exercise 8.12 Overloaded -> Operator (continued).

Exercise 8.12 displays an empty date and a real one as shown here:

0/0/0

3/17/90

An object of the **DatePtr** class is a pointer that knows whether or not a value has ever been assigned to it. If the program tries to use the pointer without first assigning the address of a **Date** object to it, the pointer contains the address of a null **Date** instead of garbage. The **DatePtr** object always returns the address of a **Date** object or the address of the null **Date** because the **DatePtr** conversion constructor function accepts no value that is not the address of a **Date**, and substitutes zero if a **DatePtr** is constructed without a parameter. When the overloaded -> operator function sees that the **dp** pointer is 0, it returns the address of the null **Date** object rather than the value in the pointer;

Note that the overloaded -> pointer operator must be a nonstatic member function. You cannot implement it as a **friend** function in the manner of other operators.

Summary

This chapter showed you how to overload C++ operators to work with your classes. As you apply these techniques try to keep a rein on your enthusiasm. You can get carried away with overloaded operators, and your code can become difficult to understand. Always overload operators in intuitive ways, and always use liberal comments in class definition header files to document the behavior of the operators you overload. One industry sage observed that C++ programmers first learn to overload operators. Then they learn not to.

Chapter 9

Class Inheritance

Class inheritance is the technique used to build new classes from old ones and to build object-oriented class hierarchies. You can build several layers of classes that are derived from other classes. You can build hierarchies of classes by using single and multiple inheritance. This chapter describes these processes by using small classes to demonstrate the features of inheritance. You will learn about:

- Base and derived classes
- Protected class members
- Public and private base classes
- Overriding base class functions
- Pointers and references to base and derived classes
- Virtual and pure virtual functions
- Polymorphism
- Virtual destructors
- Constructors and destructors in a hierarchy
- Multiple inheritance
- Virtual base classes

Base and Derived Classes

Inheritance is when you derive a new class from an existing class. The class from which you derive is called the *base* class and the new class is called the *derived* class. A base class has derived classes, each of which can be the base of other derived classes, all of which forms a class hierarchy. With multiple inheritance, a derived class can have more than one base class, each of which can have one or more base classes of its own.

A derived class inherits the characteristics of its base. The derived class automatically possesses the data members and member functions of the base. The derived class can add its own data members and member functions and it can override the member functions of the base. Adding and overriding members is how you modify the behavior of a base class to form a derived class.

There are two reasons to derive a class. One is that you want to modify the behavior of an existing class. The other is that you are building a well-organized, object-oriented class hierarchy where the user-defined data types descend from one root class. These two reasons are design approaches, but the class inheritance behavior of C++ that supports them is the same, with the same rules and boundaries.

Why use inheritance to modify the behavior of an existing class? Why not just change the base class, making it do what you want it to do? There are several reasons.

First, the base class might be used by other parts of your program and by other programs, and you want its original behavior to remain intact for those objects that already use it. By deriving a class from the base, you define a new data type that inherits all of the characteristics of the base without disturbing its purpose to the rest of the program.

Second, the source code for the base class might not be available to you. All you need to use a class are its definition and the object code for its member functions. If you are using class libraries from other sources, you might not have the source code for the member functions and you could not change it.

Third, the base class might be an abstract base class, which is designed to be a base class only. A class hierarchy can contain general-purpose classes that do nothing on their own. Their purpose is to define the behavior of some generic data structure to which derived classes add the implementation details. An abstract base list class, for example, can define the methods that manage the inserting, changing, deleting, reordering, and searching of entries in the list without defining any actual entry values. Until you derive a class that describes the data in the list, the list class does nothing.

Fourth, you might be building a class hierarchy to derive the benefits of the object-oriented approach. One of these benefits is the availability of general-purpose class methods that modify their own behavior based on the characteristics of the subclasses that use them. The class hierarchy approach supports this ability through the virtual function mechanism. You will learn about this technique later in the chapter.

Single Inheritance

You have been dealing with potential base classes since Chapter 5. All C++ structures and classes can have derived classes. The base class does not define inheritance; the derived class does. The base class has nothing in it that tells it which classes, if any, are derived from it. A derived class specifes its base.

The exercises in this book, up until now, have been independent, stand-alone programs. To learn about inheritance, you will define classes in header files, put member functions in separate class-specific source files, and link the object code compiled from those multiple source files to make running programs.

Immediately following are a header file named *timeday.h* and a source file named *timeday.cpp*. They contain the definition and implementation of a **Time** class and are similar to the class definitions that you learned in Chapter 7.

```
// Header file to define the Time class
// ---------- timeday.h

#ifndef TIMEDAY_H
#define TIMEDAY_H

#include <iostream.h>
//
// A Time Class
//
```

(continued)

```
class Time    {
    int hours, minutes, seconds;
public:
    Time(int hr, int min, int sec);
    void display();
};

#endif
```

```
// ----- timeday.cpp

#include "timeday.h"

Time::Time(int hr, int min, int sec)
{
    hours - hr;
    minutes - min;
    seconds - sec;
}
void Time::display()
{
    cout << hours << ':' << minutes << ':' << seconds;
}
```

The next two files are *date.h* and *date.cpp*, which define the **Date** class that subsequent exercises use.

```
// --------- date.h

#ifndef DATE_H
#define DATE_H

// ------ base Date class
class Date {
protected:
    int month, day, year;
public:
    Date(int m=0, int d=0, int y=0);
    void display();
};

#endif
```

```
// --------- date.cpp

#include <iostream.h>
#include "date.h"

Date::Date(int m, int d, int y)
{
    month = m;
    day = d;
    year = y;
}
void Date::display()
{
    cout << month << '/' << day << '/' << year;
}
```

Be sure to remember when you compile the exercises that use these classes to link the source files from these classes into your executable progams.

Designing a Derived Class

You haven't used the **Time** class for anything yet. Perhaps other programs use it regularly. You determine that while you need its basic properties for storing the time of day, your programs must record and report the time zone in addition to hours, minutes, and seconds. You can't modify the **Time** class because that might have impact on other programs that use it. You can, however, derive a class from it and add the new requirements.

Following are *timezone.h* and *timezone.cpp*, header and source files that define and implement the **TimeZone** class, which maintains and displays the time along with its time zone. To use your new class in an application program, you would include *timezone.h* in your source and link the compiled *timezone.cpp* with your program.

```cpp
// Header to define derived TimeZone class
// ---------- timezone.h

#ifdef TIMEZONE_H
#define TIMEZONE_H

#include "timeday.h"
//
// A TimeZone Class
//

enum timezone { gmt, est, cst, mst, pst };

class TimeZone : public Time {
    timezone zone;
protected:
    const char *Zone();
public:
    TimeZone(int hr, int min, int sec, timezone zn);
    void display();
};
```

(continued)

```
#endif

// ---------- timezone.cpp

#include "timezone.h"

static const char *TZ[] = { "GMT","EST","CST","MST","PST" };

TimeZone::TimeZone(int hr, int min, int sec, timezone zn)
            : Time(hr, min, sec)
{
    zone = zn;
}

void TimeZone::display()
{
    Time::display();
    cout << ' ' << Zone();
}

const char *TimeZone::Zone()
{
    return TZ[zone];
}
```

The **TimeZone** class is derived from the base class **Time**. You specify a base class with the colon (:) operator following the derived class name, as illustrated in the following statement:

```
class TimeZone : public Time { /* ... */ };
```

Protected Members

Observe the protected access specifier that appears ahead of the data member in *timezone.h*. You learned about public and private members in Chapter 7. Protected members behave just like private members until a new class is derived from a base class that has protected members.

If a base class has private members, those members are not accessible to the derived class. Protected members are public to derived classes but private to the rest of the program. Use of the **protected** keyword is the only acknowledgment by the **TimeZone** class in *timezone.h* that it might ever be a base class.

When you design a class, you should proceed as if the class would someday be derived, even if you have no such intentions. Specify the **protected** keyword for members that could be accessible to derived classes.

The **TimeZone** class has one protected data member, the **zone** variable. It also has, indirectly, three other data members. These are the three private data members of the **Time** class: **hours**, **minutes**, and **seconds**. But because these members are private to the **Time** class, the member functions of the **TimeZone** class cannot have access to them except through the public and protected member functions of the **Time** class.

Public and Private Base Classes

A derived class can specify that a base class is public, protected, or private by using the following notation in the definition of the derived class:

```
class TimeZone : private Time { /* ... */ };
class DispTime : public Time  { /* ... */ };
```

The **private** access specifier means that the protected and public members of the base class are private members of the derived class. The **public** access specifier means that the protected members of the base class are protected members of the derived class and the public members of the base class are public members of the derived class.

If you do not provide an access specifier, the compiler assumes that the access is **private** unless the base class is a structure, in which case the compiler assumes that the access is **public**.

Constructors in the Base and Derived Classes

When you declare an object of a derived class, the compiler executes the constructor function of the base class followed by the constructor function of the derived class.

The parameter list for the derived class's constructor function could be different from that of the base class's constructor function. Therefore, the constructor function for the derived class must tell the compiler what values to use as arguments to the constructor function for the base class.

The derived class's constructor function specifies the arguments to the base class's constructor function in *timezone.cpp* as follows:

```
TimeZone::TimeZone(int hr, int min, int sec, timezone zn)
        : Time(hr, min, sec)
```

The colon (:) operator after the derived constructor's parameter list specifies that an argument list for a base class's constructor follows. The argument list is in parentheses and follows the name of the base class.

The arguments to the constructor function of the base class are expressions that may use constants and the parameter list of the derived class's constructor function. They can be any valid C++ expressions that match the types of the base constructor's parameter list. In this case, the **TimeZone** constructor passes its arguments on to the **Time** constructor.

When a base class has more than one constructor function, the compiler decides which one to call based on the types of the arguments in the base constructor argument list as specified by the derived class constructor function.

Overriding Base Class Functions in the Derived Class

When a base and a derived class have public member functions with the same name and parameter list types, the function in the derived class overrides that in the base class when the function is called as a member of the derived class object.

Both the base **Time** class and the derived **TimeZone** class have functions named **display**. A program that declares an object of type **TimeZone** can call the **display** function for that type, and the function in the derived class object executes. Exercise 9.1 is a program that uses the derived **TimeZone** class.

```
#include "timezone.h"

main()
{
    TimeZone tz(10, 26, 0, est);
    tz.display();
}
```

Exercise 9.1 Using a Derived Class.

You must compile *timezone.cpp* and the exercise independently. Then you link them together to build the executable program.

Exercise 9.1 displays the following message:

```
10:26:0 EST
```

A program can declare objects of both the base and derived classes. The two objects are independent of one another.

Exercise 9.2 shows a program that uses **Time** and **TimeZone** objects.

```
#include <iostream.h>
#include "timezone.h"

main()
{
    Time tm(23, 15, 45);
    tm.display();
    cout << '\n';
    TimeZone tz(10, 26, 0, est);
    tz.display();
}
```

Exercise 9.2 Using a Base and a Derived Class.

Exercise 9.2 displays the following messages showing that each object uses the **display** function of its own class:

```
23:15:45
10:26:0 EST
```

Classes Derived from Derived Base Classes

You can derive a class from a base class that was itself derived from another base class. Suppose that neither the **Time** class nor the **TimeZone** class fully satisfies a new requirement.

The **Time** class maintains the 24-hour military clock. (Actually, it records and displays whatever value you care to write into the hour with your initializers. A more complete class would validate its initializers.) But suppose there is a new requirement to display the time in a 12-hour format with the time zone indicator and with am or pm notation. You can derive a class from the **TimeZone** base that incorporates the new requirements.

Following are *disptime.h* and *disptime.cpp,* header and source files that define and implement the **DispTime** class, which is derived from the **TimeZone** class.

```
// Header to define derived DispTime class
// ---------- disptime.h

#ifndef DISPTIME_H
#define DISPTIME_H

#include <stdio.h>
#include "timezone.h"


//
// A DispTime Class
//
```

(continued)

```
class DispTime : public TimeZone {
protected:
    char ampm;
public:
    DispTime(int hr, int min, int sec, timezone zn);
    void display();
};
#endif
```

```
// ---------- disptime.cpp

#include "disptime.h"

inline int adjust(int hour)
{
    return hour > 12 ? hour - 12 : (hour == 0 ? 12 : hour);
}

inline char makeampm(int hour)
{
    return hour < 12 ? 'a' : 'p';
}

DispTime::DispTime(int hr, int min, int sec, timezone zn)
            : TimeZone(adjust(hr), min, sec, zn)
```

(continued)

```
    {
        ampm = makeampm(hr);
    }
    void DispTime::display()
    {
        Time::display();
        cout << ' ' << ampm << 'm';
        cout << ' ' << Zone();
    }
```

The *disptime.cpp* source file begins with two *inline* functions. The first, **adjust**, adjusts the 0-to-24 hour value to one that is correct for a 12-hour clock. Zero becomes 12, and 13 to 23 become 1 to 11. The second **inline** function, **makeampm**, returns the letter a if the hour is less than 12, otherwise it returns p.

This use of **inline** functions shows how the **inline** keyword can replace the preprocessor's **#define** statement for macros with parameters. The **inline** format is better because it enjoys all of the notational convenience of a function declaration.

Note that the argument list for the base **TimeZone** constructor uses the **adjust** function to initialize the **hours** data member all the way up in the base **Time** class. When you use the **DispTime** class, **hours** are always 1 to 12.

The **DispTime** constructor initializes the **ampm** data member by calling the **makeampm** function with the **hr** parameter as an argument.

The class definitions for **TimeZone** and **DispTime** both have protected data members. The class definition for **Time** did not. This circumstance reflects what you are likely to run into when you deal with classes from other sources. A designer of a derived class is sensitive to how a base class definition can help the process. If you needed the data members from the **Time** class to be protected, you could always change the header file that defines **Time**. This is not a good practice. It is not wise to change code that might be in use elsewhere even if the change appears to be unobtrusive.

Exercise 9.3 is a program that uses the **DispTime** class.

```
#include "disptime.h"

main()
{
    DispTime dt(21, 42, 12, pst);
    dt.display();
}
```

Exercise 9.3 Using a Derived Class from a Derived Class.

Exercise 9.3 initializes the object with a 24-hour clock value and uses the class's **display** function to display the following message:

```
9:42:12 pm PST
```

Pointers to Base and Derived Classes

The three classes, **Time**, **TimeZone**, and **DispTime**, represent three generations in a straight line of inheritance. They all have functions named **display** that perform differently. You can use these characteristics to observe how C++ behaves with class inheritance.

A pointer to a base class can be assigned the address of one of the base's derived class objects. If the derived class overrides members of the base, the compiler associates operations made through that pointer to the base class components of the object. This means that if a derived class member overrides a base class member, the pointer ignores the override.

Exercise 9.4 is a program that has a single object of type **DispTime** and three pointers to classes, one to each of the three types.

```
#include <iostream.h>
#include "disptime.h"
main()
{
    DispTime dt(21, 42, 12, pst);
    Time     *tp = &dt;
    TimeZone *zp = &dt;
    DispTime *dp = &dt;
    tp->display();
    cout << '\n';
    zp->display();
    cout << '\n';
    dp->display();
}
```

Exercise 9.4 Pointers to Base and Derived Classes.

Exercise 9.4 displays the following messages showing that the compiler selects the member function based on the type of the pointer rather than on the type of the object:

```
9:42:12
9:42:12 PST
9:42:12 pm PST
```

Scope Resolution Operator with Base and Derived Classes

A program can use the scope resolution operator (::) to bypass the override of a member that a derived class has overridden.

Exercise 9.5 declares an object of type **DispTime** and a pointer to same.

```
#include <iostream.h>
#include "disptime.h"

main()
{
    DispTime dt(21, 42, 12, pst);
    DispTime *dp = &dt;

    // -------- use the DispTime display function
    dp->display();
    cout << '\n';
    dt.display();
    cout << '\n';
    // -------- use the TimeZone display function
    dp->TimeZone::display();
    cout << '\n';
    dt.TimeZone::display();
    cout << '\n';
    // -------- use the Time display function
    dp->Time::display();
    cout << '\n';
    dt.Time::display();
    cout << '\n';
}
```

Exercise 9.5 Global Scope Resolution in Base and Derived Classes.

Exercise 9.5 calls the **display** function of the **DispTime** class twice, once directly via the object and once through the pointer. Then it uses the scope resolution operator to specify that it intends to use the **display** function for **TimeZone**, the base class of **DispTime**. Finally, it uses the same override to call the **display** function for **Time** (the base class of **TimeZone**) which is two generations removed from the object's **DispTime** class. The program displays the following messages:

```
9:42:12 pm PST
9:42:12 pm PST
21:42:12 PST
21:42:12 PST
21:42:12
21:42:12
```

Using the global scope resolution operator without specifying a type on its left compiles a call to a global, nonmember function with the same name and parameter list. If no such function exists, the compiler issues an **error** message.

References to Base and Derived Classes

A reference to a base class can be initialized with one of the base's derived class objects. If the derived class overrides members of the base, the compiler associates operations made through that reference to the base class components of the object. If a derived class member overrides a base class member, the reference ignores the override.

Exercise 9.6 is a program that has a single object of type **DispTime** and three references to classes, one to each of the three types.

```
#include <iostream.h>
#include "disptime.h"

main()
{
    DispTime dt(21, 42, 12, pst);
    Time&      tp = dt;
    TimeZone& zp = dt;
    DispTime& dp = dt;
    tp.display();
    cout << '\n';
    zp.display();
    cout << '\n';
    dp.display();
}
```

Exercise 9.6 References to Base and Derived Classes.

Exercise 9.6 displays the same messages as Exercise 9.4 as shown here:

```
9:42:12
9:42:12 PST
9:42:12 pm PST
```

This display demonstrates that the compiler selects the member function based on the type of the reference rather than on the type of the object.

Virtual Functions

A virtual function is one that is defined in a base class and that expects to be overridden by a function in a derived class with the same name and parameter types. You saw earlier that when a pointer to a base class points to a derived class object, a call to an overridden function through the pointer calls the function that is a member of the base class rather than the one belonging to the object. A virtual function will, on the other hand, pass its calls to the matching function in a derived class when the call is made from an object of the derived class. This is true regardless of the type of the pointer or reference that calls the function.

Time Classes with Virtual Functions

For the next exercise, you will modify the header files *timeday.h*, *timezone.h*, and *disptime.h* so that the member functions named **display** in all of the classes are now virtual functions like this:

```
virtual void display();
```

This exercise reflects one of those times when you modify a class rather than derive from it. In this case, the original class is still under development, and you are improving on it.

Recompile *timeday.cpp*, *timezone.cpp*, and *disptime.cpp*. Link these compiled modules with the compiled output from Exercises 9.4 and 9.6. When you run the new programs, you see this output:

```
9:42:12 pm PST
9:42:12 pm PST
9:42:12 pm PST
```

When you compare these messages with those displayed by Exercises 9.4 and 9.6, you can see that the compiler now elects to use the **display** function in the **DispTime** class even when the reference is to the type **Time** or **TimeZone**.

Overriding the Virtual Function Override

If you want a virtual function to execute even when the calling object has an overriding function, you can use the scope resolution operator (::) to specify that the virtual function is to execute.

Exercise 9.7 modifies the program from Exercise 9.6 so that the virtual **TimeZone::display** function executes, even though the **DispTime** object has an overriding display function.

```
#include <iostream.h>
#include "disptime.h"

main()
{
    DispTime dt(21, 42, 12, pst);
    Time&     tp = dt;
    TimeZone& zp = dt;
    DispTime& dp = dt;
    tp.Time::display();
    cout << '\n';
    zp.TimeZone::display();
    cout << '\n';
    dp.display();
}
```

Exercise 9.7 Overriding the Virtual Function Override.

The modified program in Exercise 9.7 displays the same messages that Exercise 9.4 displayed and that Exercise 9.6 displayed before you made the display functions in the classes virtual as shown here:

```
9:42:12
9:42:12 PST
9:42:12 pm PST
```

Virtual Functions Without Derived Overrides

If the derived class has no function to override the base class's virtual function, then the base class's function executes regardless of the pointer or reference type.

Exercise 9.8 derives a class from **Time** to demonstrate that a virtual function in a base class executes if the derived class of the invoking object has no overriding function.

```
#include <iostream.h>

#include "timeday.h"

class NewTime : public Time    {
public:
    NewTime(int hr,int min,int sec) : Time(hr,min,sec)
        { /* empty */ }
};
class MoreTime : public NewTime    {
public:
    MoreTime(int hr,int min,int sec) : NewTime(hr,min,sec)
        { /* empty */ }
};
main()
{
    MoreTime dt(21, 42, 12);
    NewTime *nt = &dt;
    Time& tp = dt;

    dt.display();
    cout << '\n';
    tp.display();
    cout << '\n';
    nt->display();
    cout << '\n';
}
```

Exercise 9.8 Virtual Function with no Derived Override.

Neither the **NewTime** class nor the **MoreTime** class in Exercise 9.8 has a **display** function to override the virtual **display** function of the **Time** class. Therefore, all three calls to the **display** function execute the virtual function in the **Time** class, and the program displays the following messages:

```
21:42:12
21:42:12
21:42:12
```

Pure Virtual Functions

A base class can specify a pure virtual function, which means that the base class is a virtual base class. The base class provides no function body for the pure virtual function. In this case, the program may not declare any objects of the base class and a derived class must declare the function. A class derived directly from the base does not have to declare the function as long as somewhere down the class hierarchy a lower derived class declares it.

The following code shows you how to specify a pure virtual function:

```
class Time {
  // ...
public:
    virtual void display() = 0;
}
```

The zero initializer identifies the function as a pure virtual function. The class may not supply a function body, and a program may not declare an object of the base class.

Exercise 9.9 modifies the program in Exercise 9.8 by specifying a pure virtual display function for the **Time** class and by replacing the **display** function in the **TimeZone** class.

```
#include <iostream.h>

#include "timeday.h"

class NewTime : public Time    {
public:
    NewTime(int hr,int min,int sec) : Time(hr,min,sec)
        { /* empty */ }
    virtual void Showit() = 0;
};
class MoreTime : public NewTime    {
public:
    MoreTime(int hr,int min,int sec) : NewTime(hr,min,sec)
        { /* empty */ }
    void Showit() { display(); }
};
main()
{
    MoreTime dt(21, 42, 12);
    NewTime *nt = &dt;

    dt.Showit();
    cout << '\n';
    nt->Showit();
    cout << '\n';
}
```

Exercise 9.9 Pure Virtual Function.

The program in Exercise 9.9 derives a **NewTime** class from the base **Time** class. The **NewTime** class has a pure virtual function named **Showit**. The main function declares an object of type **MoreTime** and a pointer to type **NewTime**, which contains the address of the **MoreTime** object. The program calls the

Showit function directly for the object and then through the pointer. In both cases, the **MoreTime::Showit** function is called. It calls **display**, which is a public member function of the base **Time** class. Exercise 9.9 displays the following messages:

```
21:42:12
21:42:12
```

Virtual Functions and Multiple Derived Classes

If a base class has multiple derived classes, and more than one of them overrides a virtual function, the compiler selects the function from the class for which the calling object is declared.

Exercise 9.10 defines an abstract **Date** class and two derived classes, **NumDate** and **AlphaDate**. The **Date** class has a pure virtual function named **display** which is overridden by **display** functions in the derived classes.

```cpp
#include <iostream.h>

// --------- abstract date class
class Date {
protected:
    int mo, da, yr;
public:
    Date(int m, int d, int y)
        {mo = m; da = d; yr = y;}
    virtual void display() = 0;
};

// --------- derived numeric date class
class NumDate : public Date {
public:
```

Exercise 9.10 Virtual Functions and Multiple Derived Classes.

```
    NumDate(int m, int d, int y) : Date(m, d, y)
        { /* ... */ }
    void display()
    { cout << mo << '/' << da << '/' << yr; }
};

// -------- derived alphabetic date class
class AlphaDate : public Date {
public:
    AlphaDate(int m, int d, int y) : Date(m, d, y)
        { /* ... */ }
    void display();
};
// ------ Display function for AlphaDate
void AlphaDate::display()
{
    static char *mos[] = {
        "January","February","March","April",
        "May","June","July",August",
        "September","October","November","December"
    };
    cout << mos[mo-1] << ' ' << da << ", " << yr+1900;
}

main()
{
    NumDate nd(7,29,41);
    AlphaDate ad(11,17,41);

    Date& dt1 = nd;
```

Exercise 9.10 Virtual Functions and Multiple Derived Classes (continued).

```
        Date& dt2 = ad;
        dt1.display();
        cout << '\n';
        dt2.display();
    }
```

Exercise 9.10 Virtual Functions and Multiple Derived Classes (continued).

The program in Exercise 9.10 declares objects of types **NumDate** and **AlphaDate**. The two dates have different initialized values so you can tell them apart. Then the program declares two references to **Date** objects, initializing one to refer to the **NumDate** object and the other to refer to the **AlphaDate** object. The important point is that both references as defined refer to the base class, but as initialized they refer to the derived class objects.

The program calls the **display** function by using the **Date** references and displays the following messages:

```
7/29/41
November 17, 1941
```

When the program calls the **display** function through a reference to the **Date** class, the compiler must select a function to execute. Because the **display** function in the **Date** class is virtual, the compiler selects the **display** function for the object to which the **Date** reference refers.

Polymorphism

Polymorbism is the ability for different objects in a class hierarchy to exhibit unique behavior in response to the same message. **Employee** and **Contractor** classes derived from a base **Worker** class, for example, can have different behavior even when a message is sent to their objects through a reference to their base **Worker** class.

In the next exercise you have a string of base and derived classes like the following:

```
OrgEntity - Company - Division - Department
```

OrgEntity is the root base, and **Department** is the lowest derived class. The **OrgEntity** class is an abstract class, which means its sole purpose is to be a base class. It has a function named **number_employees**, and every class in the hierarchy has a virtual function named **office_party**. The functions return the variable number of employees assigned to each organizational entity and a constant amount per employee budgeted for the annual office party.

Following are *org.h* and *org.cpp*, the header and source files that define and implement these four base and derived classes. The files contain code to support several subsequent exercises.

```
// ------------ org.h

#ifndef ORG_H
#define ORG_H

#include <iostream.h>
#include <string.h>

class OrgEntity {
    char name[25];
    int employee_count;
public:
    OrgEntity(char *s, int ec);
    int number_employees()
        { return employee_count; }
    char *org_name()
        { return name; }
    virtual int office_party() = 0;
};

class Company : public OrgEntity    {
public:
```

(continued)

```
        Company(char *s, int ec);
        virtual int office_party();
    };

    class Division : public Company    {
    public:
        Division(char *s, int ec);
        virtual int office_party();
    };

    class Department : public Division    {
    public:
        Department(char *s, int ec);
        int office_party();
    };

    #endif
```

```
    // ------- org.cpp

    #include "org.h"

    OrgEntity::OrgEntity(char *s, int ec)
    {
        strcpy(name, s);
        employee_count = ec;
    }

    Company::Company(char *s, int ec) : OrgEntity(s, ec)
    {
```

(continued)

```
    // empty constructor
}

int Company::office_party()
{
    return 100;
}

Division::Division(char *s, int ec) : Company(s, ec)
{
    // empty constructor
}

int Division::office_party()
{
    return 75;
}

Department::Department(char *s, int ec) : Division(s, ec)
{
    // empty constructor
}

int Department::office_party()
{
    return 50;
}
```

It might appear that the three lower classes in *org.h* could each simply derive from the **OrgEntity** base class. So they could, but, while not shown in the exercise, in actual practice such classes would contain other specialized and inherited members related to the organizational entities they represent. Tiered layers of inheritance would, therefore, be appropriate.

Somewhere in the organization's accounting system is a budget management process that generates annual budget reports. It does not necessarily know what kind of organizational entity it is working with at the time, so it must rely on the design of the class hierarchy to cause each class to behave in its own unique way.

Exercise 9.11 is a program that emulates this relationship. The main function stubs the exercise by declaring objects of the classes and calling the **budget** function for each one.

```
#include <iostream.h>
#include "org.h"

void budget(OrgEntity& oe);

main()
{
    Company company("Bilbo Software, Inc.", 35);
    Division div("Vertical Applications", 12);
    Department dept("Medical Practice", 4);
    budget(company);
    budget(div);
    budget(dept);
}

void budget(OrgEntity& oe)
{
    cout << "\n---- Budget Report ----\n";
    cout << oe.org_name();
    cout << " $" << oe.number_employees() * oe.office_party();
    cout << '\n';
}
```

Exercise 9.11 A Company's Budget Program.

The **budget** function represents a part of a software system that does not necessarily know which of the classes it is dealing with that are derived from **OrgEntity**. The virtual **office_party** function represents a way that each derived class can provide its own specialized behavior for a given process. The program displays the following messages:

```
---- Budget Report ----
Bilbo Software, Inc. $3500
---- Budget Report ----
Vertical Applications $900
---- Budget Report ----
Medical Practice $200
```

This ability for each derived class to provide its own custom version of a general function and for the compiler to select the correct one based on the object being processed, is called polymorphism in the object-oriented lexicon. Chapter 13 explains polymorphism in more detail.

Virtual Destructors

When an object of a derived class goes out of scope, the destructor for the derived class executes and then the destructor for the base class executes. There are potential problems in this process, however. If the destructor executes as the result of the **delete** operator and if the pointer type is the base class, the base destructor executes instead of the derived destructor.

Exercise 9.12 illustrates this destructor-execution behavior in base and derived classes.

```
#include <iostream.h>
#include <string.h>

// ------------- OrgEntity Class
class OrgEntity {
```

Exercise 9.12 Base and Derived Destructors.

```
    char *name;
public:
    OrgEntity(char *s);
    ~OrgEntity();
    void org_name();
};
OrgEntity::OrgEntity(char *s)
{
    name = new char[strlen(s)+1];
    strcpy(name, s);
}
OrgEntity::~OrgEntity()
{
    cout << "\nOrgEntity destructor";
    delete name;
}
void OrgEntity::org_name()
{
    cout << name;
}
// ------------ Division Class
class Division : public OrgEntity  {
    char *manager;
public:
    Division(char *s, char *mgr);
    ~Division();
};
Division::Division(char *s, char *mgr) : OrgEntity(s)
{
```

Exercise 9.12 Base and Derived Destructors (continued).

```
    manager=new char[strlen(mgr)+1];
    strcpy(manager, mgr);
}
Division::~Division()
{
    cout << "\nDivision destructor";
    delete manager;
}

main()
{
    OrgEntity *orgs[3];
    orgs[0] = new OrgEntity("Bilbo Software, Inc.");
    orgs[1] = new Division("Vert Apps", "Ron Herold");
    orgs[2] = new Division("Horiz Apps", "Bob Young");
    for (int i = 0; i < 3; i++)    {
        // ....... process the organization objects
        delete orgs[i]; // not always right destructor
    }
}
```

Exercise 9.12 Base and Derived Destructors (continued).

When you design a class hierarchy, you must consider each method with respect to whether or not it should be a virtual function. If you are defining a member function whose method is specific to the class, you must ask if any derived class might have a similar function with the same name. The **display** function you have seen in many exercises in this book is a good example of a general-purpose function whose operation could be overridden by a derived class. Next, you must ask whether calls of the function are always in the name of the actual object or whether they might be through a pointer or reference to a base class. Answering that, you must determine whether such calls need the services of the function that is a member of the pointer/reference class or whether they need a virtual function that finds its way to the member function of the actual class of which the object is a type. These are the kinds of decisions that face the designer of an object-oriented class hierarchy.

Exercise 9.12 has a base **OrgEntity** class and a derived **Division** class. Both classes have destructors because they both contain pointer data members that are initialized with free store-memory by their constructors. Both classes should also have copy constructors and overloaded assignment operators for the same reason, which you learned about in Chapter 7.

The destructor functions of both classes display messages to show that they are executing, and they both delete the free-store memory to which their member pointers point.

The main function declares an array of pointers to the **OrgEntity** class, initializes one of them with a pointer to a new **OrgEntity** object, and initializes the other two with pointers to new **Division** objects. Because these objects were built by the **new** operator, they must be destroyed by the **delete** operator.

The main function uses a **for** loop to process and delete the objects. However, the pointers in the array are **OrgEntity** types, so the **delete** operator calls the destructor function for the **OrgEntity** class even when the pointer points to a **Division** object. The result is that the free-store memory allocated to the two **Division** class objects for their manager members never gets deleted. Exercise 9.12 displays the following messages to prove that only the **OrgEntity** destructor ever gets called:

```
OrgEntity destructor
OrgEntity destructor
OrgEntity destructor
```

The solution to the problem revealed by Exercise 9.12 is to declare the destructor function for the base class to be virtual. When a base class destructor is virtual, all of the destructors below it in the hierarchy are automatically virtual, and the compiler can call the correct destructor function.

Note that while destructor functions can be virtual, constructor functions cannot be virtual.

Change the **OrgEntity** destructor prototype in the class definition in Exercise 9.12 to a virtual destructor like this:

```
virtual ~OrgEntity();
```

Following that change, the program displays the following messages:

```
OrgEntity destructor
Division destructor
OrgEntity destructor
Division destructor
OrgEntity destructor
```

The first **OrgEntity** destructor message comes when the program deletes the **OrgEntity** object. The next two pairs of messages, **Division** destructor, **OrgEntity** destructor, come when the program deletes the two **Division** objects.

Multiple Inheritance

Multiple inheritance is when a derived class has more than one base class. It allows you to define a new class that inherits the characteristics of several unrelated base classes.

You specify more than one base class when you define a derived class with multiple inheritance. The following notation defines a **FileStamp** class derived from the **Time** and **Date** classes:

```
class FileStamp : public Time, public Date {
    // ...
};
```

The constructor function declaration in a class derived from multiple bases specifies the arguments for the constructors of all of the base classes as shown here:

```
FileStamp::Filestamp(int dd,int mm,int yy,
                          int hr,int mn,int sc)
    : Time(hr, mn, sc), Date(mm, dd, yy)
```

Exercise 9.13 is a program that derives the **FileStamp** class from two bases, the **Time** class and the **Date** class. In this exercise, the **FileStamp** class records the date and time when something happens to a file. It has its own data member to store the name of the file, and it uses the properties it inherits from the **Date** and **Time** classes to manage the date and time.

```
#include <iostream.h>
#include <string.h>
#include "timeday.h"
#include "date.h"

// ------ derived FileStamp class
class FileStamp : public Time, public Date    {
protected:
    char filename[15];
public:
    FileStamp(char *fn, int mm, int dd, int yy,
                       int hr, int mn, int sc);
    void display();
};

FileStamp::FileStamp(char *fn, int mm, int dd, int yy,
                            int hr, int mn, int sc)
        : Time(hr, mn, sc), Date(mm, dd, yy)
{
    strcpy(filename, fn);
}

void FileStamp::display()
{
    cout << filename << ' ';
    Date::display();
    cout << ' ';
```

Exercise 9.13 Multiple Inheritance.

```
    Time::display();
}

main()
{
    FileStamp fs("DATAFILE", 4, 6, 90, 13, 32, 27);
    fs.display();
}
```

Exercise 9.13 Multiple Inheritance (continued).

The **Date** and **Time** classes each have **display** functions to display their contents. The **FileStamp** function overrides those functions with its own **display** function. The **FileStamp::display** function uses the virtual display functions of the two base classes by using the scope resolution operator to call them.

Exercise 9.13 displays the following message:

```
DATAFILE 4/6/90 13:32:27
```

Ambiguities with Multiple Inheritance

Suppose that the **FileStamp** class in Exercise 9.13 had no **display** function to override the **virtual** display functions of the two base classes. This would not be a problem as long as the program did not attempt to call the **display** function through an object of type **FileStamp**, or a pointer or reference to one. If it did, however, the program would not compile because the compiler would not know which of the two **display** functions to execute. The program can resolve this ambiguity by using the scope resolution operator to specify which class's **display** function to use, as shown in the following example:

```
fs.Date::display();
```

The same ambiguities can exist with data members. If both base classes have data members with the same name and the derived class has no such data member, the member functions of the derived class must use the scope resolution operator to resolve which base class's data member to use.

If the data members are public, the program cannot access such an ambiguous data member directly through the object, but must use the scope resolution operator and the base class name in the same manner that is shown for member functions above.

Constructor Execution with Multiple Inheritance

When the program declares an object of a class that is derived from multiple bases, the constructors for the base classes are called first. The order of execution is the order in which the base classes are declared as bases to the derived class. Consider the following example:

```
class FileStamp : public Time, public Date {
    // ...
};
```

The constructor for the **Time** class executes first followed by the constructor for the **Date** class. The constructor for the **FileStamp** class executes last.

If the class definition includes another class as a member, that class's constructor executes after the constructors for the base classes and before the constructor for the class being defined. Consider the following example:

```
class Name { /* ... */ };
class FileStamp : public Time, public Date {
    Name filename;
    // ...
};
```

The order of constructor execution is **Time**, **Date**, **Name**, and **FileStamp**.

Destructor Execution with Multiple Inheritance

When an object of a class goes out of scope, the destructors execute in the reverse order of the constructors.

Virtual Base Classes

Multiple inheritance has the potential for a derived class to have too many instances of one of the bases. Consider the following structure:

```
class BillingItem {
protected:
    char name[25];
    int cost;
public:
    virtual void display() = 0;
};
```

The **BillingItem** class is an abstract base class that is the base class for two derived classes in a system that supports the sale of products and services. The following are the derived classes:

```
class Product : public BillingItem {
protected:
    int qty_sold;
public:
    Product(char *nm, int qty, int cst)
        { qty_sold = qty; }
    void display() { cout << qty_sold; }
};
class Service : public BillingItem {
protected:
    int manhours;
public:
    Service(char *nm, int mh, int cst)
        { manhours = mh; }
    void display() { cout << manhours; }
};
```

A program that declares an object of either of these classes has access to the name and cost data members of the base **BillingItem** class. That, combined with the **display** functions of the derived classes, gives the program the ability to report the details of individual product and service sales.

Suppose that the system also needs to support the sale of installed products where the sale involves a number of products and the labor hours to perform the installation. It is reasonable to want to build a new class that inherits the characteristics of the two existing classes. Such a new class is shown as follows:

```
class Installation : public Product, public Service     {
public:
    Installation(char *nm, int qty, int hrs, int cst)
        : Product(nm, qty, cst), Service(nm, hrs, cst)   { }
    void display();
};
```

A problem arises because the **Product** and **Service** classes are both derived from the **BillingItem** class, therefore, the **Installation** class inherits two copies of it. You do not want that to happen. An installation is one billing item with one name and one cost. It does not need two representations of these data members. Furthermore, any attempt to address **name** or **cost** for an **Installation** object would result in a compile-time ambiguity that the program could resolve only by applying the scope resolution operator to associate the member with one of the intermediate base classes.

C++ allows you to specify in the definition of a derived class that a base class is virtual. As a result, all virtual occurrences of the class throughout the class hierarchy share one actual occurrence of it. To specify a virtual base class, use the following notation:

```
class Product : public virtual BillingItem {
    // ...
};
```

There are rules, however, about how a virtual base class can itself be specified. A class that uses a constructor that accepts parameters cannot be a virtual base class. If this restriction did not exist, the compiler would not know which constructor argument list from which derived class to use.

A pointer to a virtual base class cannot be cast to a class that is derived from it, either directly or further down the class hierarchy.

N O T E

Exercise 9.14 shows the use of a virtual base class such as the one just discussed.

```
#include <iostream.h>
#include <string.h>

class BillingItem    {
protected:
    char name[25];
    int cost;
public:
    virtual void display() - 0;
};

class Product : public virtual BillingItem    {
    int qty_sold;
public:
    Product(char *nm, int qty, int cst);
    void display();
};
Product::Product(char *nm, int qty, int cst)
{
    qty_sold - qty;
    strcpy(name, nm);
    cost - cst;
}
void Product::display()
```

Exercise 9.14 Virtual Base Classes.

```
{
    cout << qty_sold;
}

class Service : public virtual BillingItem    {
    int manhours;
public:
    Service(char *nm, int mh, int cst);
    void display();
};

Service::Service(char *nm, int mh, int cst)
{
    manhours = mh;
    strcpy(name, nm);
    cost = cst;
}
void Service::display()
{
    cout << manhours;
}

class Installation : public Product, public Service    {
public:
    Installation(char *nm, int qty, int hrs, int cst)
        : Product(nm, qty, cst), Service(nm, hrs, cst) { }
    void display();
};
void Installation::display()
{
```

Exercise 9.14 Virtual Base Classes (continued).

```
        cout << "\nInstalled ";
        Product::display();
        cout << ' ' << name << 's';
        cout << "\nLabor: ";
        Service::display();
        cout << " hours";
        cout << "\nCost: $" << cost;
    }
    main()
    {
        Installation inst("refrigerator", 2, 3, 75);
        inst.display();
    }
```

Exercise 9.14 Virtual Base Classes.

Both the **Product** and the **Service** class definitions specify that the **BillingItem** base class is virtual. Observe that the constructors for these two classes take care of initializing the data members for the **BillingItem** class because it does not have a constructor with a parameter list. The **Installation** class is derived from the **Product** and **Service** classes.

The main function declares an **Installation** object, initializes it with some values, and uses its **display** function to display the following messages:

```
Installed 2 refrigerators
Labor: 3 hours
Cost: $75
```

Summary

There is more than just language to know about the C++ language development environment. Along with implementations of the language comes a library of standard stream input/output classes and functions. You have already used that library extensively by including *iostream.h* in the exercises and using the **cin** and **cout** objects to read and write the console. Chapter 10 is about C++ input/output streams and how you can use their advanced features for file input/output as well as for the console.

C++ Input/Output Streams

The exercises in this book have used the C++ **iostream** class library to read input from the keyboard and display results on the screen. The **iostream** class library has capabilities beyond those that read and write the console, however. The library is the C++ equivalent to the standard C stream input/output functions, and you can use it to manage console and file input/output.

The **iostream** classes have more features than this chapter describes. After mastering the usages in the exercises given here, you should refer to the **iostream** documentation that comes with your compiler to see how to use its more advanced features. This chapter provides sufficient knowledge to use the streams in the ways that support most programming problems. You will learn:

- Input and output stream classes
- Buffered and formatted output
- put and write member functions
- get, getline, and read member functions
- Overloading << and >>
- File input/output

C++ has no input/output operators as intrinsic or integral parts of the language. Just as C relies on function libraries to extend the language with input/output functions, C++ depends on class libraries for its input and output.

Versions of C++ prior to 2.0 included the **stream** class library, and that library is documented in the first edition of Stroustrup's *The C++ Programming Language*. (See the bibliography at the end of this book.) Some of the books that predate version 2.0 of C++ also deal with the earlier **stream** classes only.

C++ Version 2.0 and later use the improved **iostream** class library. Most of those compilers also include support for the stream library so that programs developed with earlier versions are compatible with the newer compiler. Those programs included the *stream.h* header file while users of 2.0 and greater include *iostream.h* and others to use the improved classes.

Some compilers support both generations of **stream** classes from within the *iostream.h* header file. Those compilers use the *stream.h* file name as an alias for the *iostream.h* name so that older programs compile without modification. Other compilers provide both header files.

C++ manages file and console input and output as streams of characters. C++ programs manage data values as data types such as integers, structures, classes, and so on. The **iostream** library provides the interface between the data types that a program views and the character streams of the input/output system.

Most of the exercises in this book include the *iostream.h* header file. You can learn a lot about the design of class hierarchies by reading this file. You can also answer some of your own questions about the use of the streams by looking at how they are implemented in the header file.

When the first edition of this book was written, the **iostream** class library was relatively new. Different compiler vendors implemented it according to their own interpretations of the AT&T specification. As a general rule, the implementations are consistent because the AT&T implementation was a good baseline. Until a formal standard is published, however, there are bound to be differences.

The exercises in this chapter reflect the results from the Borland, Comeau, Microsoft, and Zortech C++ **iostream** implementations. This book tells you where those products differ.

Streams

Chapter 1 introduced the C++ **iostream** class library and showed some of the ways to use it. That introduction allowed you to proceed with the exercises in this book, most of which use console input/output. Without knowing about C++ classes, you were not prepared to understand how the classes and their objects are implemented. Now that you have classes, overloaded operators, and inheritance under your belt, you are ready to learn to use the features of the **iostream** libraries.

The *ios* Class

C++ streams are implemented as classes. The **cout** and **cin** objects are instances of those classes, which derive from a base class named **ios**. There is not much to know about **ios**, although later you will use the enum values that **ios** defines. A program deals mostly with objects of types that are derived from the **ios** class.

The ostream Class

Stream output is managed by a class named **ostream**, which is derived from **ios**. You learned to display a message on the screen with a statement such as the following one:

```
cout << "Hello, Dolly";
```

The **cout** object is an external object of the **ostream** class. The **cout** object is declared in the library, and an **extern** declaration of it appears in *ostream.h* so that it is available to be used by any program that includes *iostream.h*.

Besides **cout**, *ostream.h* declares other objects as instances of the **ostream** class. The **cerr** object writes to the standard error device and uses unbuffered output. The **clog** object also writes to the standard error device, but it uses buffered output. A later part of this chapter describes buffered output.

A program writes to an **ostream** object by using the overloaded << insertion operator. The exercises in this book have used this feature extensively. The **ostream** class provides sufficient overloaded << insertion operators to support writing most standard C++ data types to the output stream. Later you will learn how to overload the << insertion operator to write your own classes to an **ostream** object.

The *istream* Class

The **istream** class manages stream input the way the **ostream** class manages output. It is externally declared in *ostream.h*. The **cin** object reads data values from the standard input device.

The **istream** class uses the overloaded >> extraction operator to read input. There are sufficient overloaded extraction >> operators to support reading the standard C++ data types, and a user-defined class can overload the >> extraction operator to read data from an **istream** object. You will learn how to do this later.

The *iostream* Class

The **iostream** class is derived from the **istream** and **ostream** classes. A program uses it for the declaration of objects that do both input and output. You do not often need to deal with the **iostream** class in basic input/output operations. The **fstream** class, which manages file input/output, derives from the **iostream** class, and that is as close as most programmers need to come to **iostream**.

Buffered Output

The data characters written to an **ostream** object are usually buffered. For example, the **ostream** class collects output bytes into a buffer and does not write them to the actual device associated with the object until one of the following events occurs: the buffer fills, the program tells the object to flush its buffer, the program terminates, or, if the output object is **cout**, the program reads data from the **cin** object. The **cout** and **clog** objects use buffered output. The **cerr** object does not.

Exercise 10.1 displays a "please wait" message, which does some extensive processing—in this case just a five-second wait loop—and then proceeds.

```
#include <iostream.h>
#include <time.h>

main()
{
    time_t tm = time(0) + 5;
    cout << "Please wait...";
    while (time(0) < tm)
        ;
    cout << "\nAll done";
}
```

Exercise 10.1 A Buffered Stream Object.

The "please wait" message does not always display when it should, because **cout** is a buffered object.

NOTE Not all compilers exhibit the same behavior. The Borland C++ compiler displays the "please wait" message immediately. The Microsoft, Comeau, and Zortech C++ compilers wait until the timer loop expires and the "\nAll done" message flushes the buffer.

The solution is to tell **cout** to flush itself as soon as you want the message to display. A program tells an **ostream** object to flush itself by sending it the **flush** manipulator.

Exercise 10.2 uses the **flush** manipulator to cause the program in Exercise 10.1 to work the way it is intended.

```
#include <iostream.h>
#include <time.h>

main()
{
    time_t tm = time(0) + 5;
    cout << "Please wait..." << flush;
    while (time(0) < tm)
        ;
    cout << "\nAll done";
}
```

Exercise 10.2 Flushing a Buffered Stream.

Formatted Output

Chapter 1 included discussions on the **dec**, **oct**, and **hex** manipulators. These manipulators set the default format for input and output. If you insert the **hex** manipulator into the output stream, for example, the object correctly translates the internal data representation of the object into the correct display. Exercise 1.6 in Chapter 1 demonstrated this behavior.

Output width

Objects of type **ostream** write data without padding as a default. The exercises in this book insert the space character between data values in the output stream to separate them. You might want some displays to be lined up in columns, which means that displays need to be written with a fixed width.

A program can specify a default width for every item displayed by inserting the **setw** manipulator into the stream or by calling the **width** member function. The **setw** manipulator and the **width** member function both take a width parameter.

Exercise 10.3 is a program that displays a column of numbers.

```
#include <iostream.h>

main()
{
    cout.unsetf(ios::scientific);
    cout.setf(ios::fixed);
    static double values[] =
        { 1.23, 35.36, 653.7, 4358.224 };
    for (int i = 0; i < 4; i++)
        cout << values[i] << '\n';
}
```

Exercise 10.3 Displaying Columns of Numbers.

Exercise 10.3 displays the following output:

```
1.23
35.36
653.7
4358.224
```

Note that the Microsoft C++ and Comeau C++ implementations pad the decimal places with zeros as shown here:

```
1.230000
35.360000
653.700000
4358.224000
```

Observe the calls to the **unsetf** and **setf** member functions for the **cout** object. These calls clear and set flags that are related to the object and that control output format. The **scientific** flag, which this exercise clears, formats a **double** or **float** output with exponential notation. The **fixed** flag formats the output with decimal positions. The default flag is **scientific**.

Exercise 10.4 demonstrates how the **width** member function manages output width. By calling the **width** function with an argument of 10, the program specifies that the displays are to appear in a column at least 10 characters wide.

```
#include <iostream.h>

main()
{
    cout.setf(ios::fixed, ios::scientific);
    static double values[] = { 1.23, 35.36, 653.7, 4358.224 };
    for (int i = 0; i < 4; i++)    {
        cout.width(10);
        cout << values[i] << '\n';
    }
}
```

*Exercise 10.4 The **width** Member Function.*

Exercise 10.4 displays the following output:

```
      1.23
     35.36
     653.7
   4358.22
```

The **setf** call in Exercise 10.4 differs from the one in Exercise 10.3. This variation on the call has two parameters, the *flag* to set and a *mask* that defines the flags to clear.

Sometimes a report needs to use different widths for different data elements, and it is convenient to insert width commands into the stream. The **setw** manipulator provides this capability.

Exercise 10.5 demonstrates the use of the **setw** manipulator to display columns that have data elements with different width requirements.

```
#include <iostream.h>
#include <iomanip.h>

main()
{
    cout.setf(ios::fixed, ios::scientific);
    static double values[] =
        { 1.23, 35.36, 653.7, 4358.224 };
    static char *names[] =
        {"Zoot", "Jimmy", "Al", "Stan"};
    for (int i = 0; i < 4; i++)
        cout << setw(6)  << names[i]
             << setw(10) << values[i] << '\n';
}
```

*Exercise 10.5 The **setw** Manipulator.*

You must include *iomanip.h* to use the **setw** manipulator.

Exercise 10.5 displays the following output:

```
Zoot       1.23
Jimmy     35.36
Al         653.7
Stan    4358.224
```

Note that using **setw** or **width** does not cause any truncation. If the data value being displayed is wider than the current width value, the entire data value still displays. You should be aware of this behavior when you design well-formatted displays that use the **setw** manipulator or the **width** member function.

Note also that the default width you specify applies only to the object for which you specified it and not for other objects of the class.

To return the object to the default width, use the **width** member function or the **setw** manipulator with a zero argument.

You can use the **fill** member function to set the value of the padding character for output that has other than the default width.

Exercise 10.6 demonstrates this usage by padding a column of numbers with asterisks.

```
#include <iostream.h>

main()
{
    cout.setf(ios::fixed, ios::scientific);
    static double values[] =
        { 1.23, 35.36, 653.7, 4358.224 };
    for (int i = 0; i < 4; i++)     {
        cout.width(10);
        cout.fill('*');
        cout << values[i] << '\n';
    }
}
```

*Exercise 10.6 The **fill** Member Function.*

Exercise 10.6 displays the following output:

```
******1.23
*****35.36
*****653.7
**4358.224
```

Output Justification

Suppose that you want the names in Exercise 10.5 to be left-justified and the number to remain right-justified. You can use the **setiosflags** manipulator to specify that the output is to be left- or right-justified.

Exercise 10.7 demonstrates **setiosflags** by modifying the display from Exercise 10.5 so that the names are left-justified.

```
#include <iostream.h>
#include <iomanip.h>

main()
{
    cout.setf(ios::fixed, ios::scientific);
    static double values[] =
        { 1.23, 35.36, 653.7, 4358.224 };
    static char *names[] =
        {"Zoot", "Jimmy", "Al", "Stan"};
    for (int i = 0; i < 4; i++)
        cout << setiosflags(ios::left)
             << setw(6)  << names[i]
             << resetiosflags(ios::left)
             << setiosflags(ios::right)
             << setw(10) << values[i] << '\n';
}
```

*Exercise 10.7 The **setiosflags** and **resetiosflags** Manipulators.*

Exercise 10.7 displays the following output:

```
Zoot        1.23
Jimmy      35.36
Al         653.7
Stan     4358.224
```

The exercise sets the left-justification flag by using the **setiosflags** manipulator with an argument of **ios::left**. This argument is an **enum** value that is defined in the **ios** class, so its reference must include the **ios::** prefix. The **resetiosflags** manipulator turns off the left-justification flag to return to the default right-justification mode.

 The Zortech 3.1 compiler does not correctly process the **ios::left** flag, and the displays from Exercises 10.7, 10.8, and 10.9 are not what you see here.

Precision

Suppose you wanted the floating point numbers in Exercise 10.7 to display with only one decimal place. The **setprecision** manipulator tells the object to use a specified number of digits of precision.

Exercise 10.8 adds the **setprecision** manipulator to the program.

```
#include <iostream.h>
#include <iomanip.h>
main()
{
    static double values[] = { 1.23, 35.36, 653.7, 4358.224 };
    static char *names[] = {"Zoot", "Jimmy", "Al", "Stan"};
    for (int i = 0; i < 4; i++)
        cout << setiosflags(ios::left)
            << setw(6)
            << names[i]
            << resetiosflags(ios::left)
            << setiosflags(ios::right)
            << setw(10)
            << setprecision(1)
            << values[i]
            << '\n';
}
```

*Exercise 10.8 The **setprecision** Manipulator.*

Exercise 10.8 displays the following output:

```
Zoot          1.2
Jimmy         35.4
Al          6.5e+02
Stan        4.4e+03
```

The scientific notation displayed by Exercise 10.8 might not be what the program needs to display. There are two flags, **ios::fixed** and **ios::scientific**, that control how a floating point number displays. A program can set and clear these flags with the **setiosflags** and **resetiosflags** manipulators.

The Microsoft C++ and Comeau C++ compilers display the values as shown here:

```
Zoot             1
Jimmy       4e+001
Al          7e+002
Stan        4e+003
```

Exercise 10.9 uses the **setiosflags** manipulator to set the **ios::fixed** flag so that the program does not display in scientific notation.

```
#include <iostream.h>
#include <iomanip.h>

main()
{
    static double values[] = { 1.23, 35.36, 653.7, 4358.224 };
    static char *names[] = {"Zoot", "Jimmy", "Al", "Stan"};
    for (int i = 0; i < 4; i++)
        cout << setiosflags(ios::left)
             << setw(6)
```

*Exercise 10.9 Setting the **ios::fixed** Flag.*

```
                    << names[i]
                    << resetiosflags(ios::left)
                    << setiosflags(ios::fixed)
                    << setiosflags(ios::right)
                    << setw(10)
                    << setprecision(1)
                    << values[i]
                    << '\n';
    }
```

*Exercise 10.9 Setting the **ios::fixed** Flag (continued).*

Exercise 10.9 displays the following output:

```
    Zoot        1.2
    Jimmy      35.4
    Al        653.7
    Stan     4358.2
```

Manipulators, Flags, and Member Functions

The exercises in this discussion have used manipulators and member functions to change the various modes of display, which are controlled by flags. The **ios** class keeps the current settings of the flags in member data items. The class defines the mnemonic values for the settings in an **enum** data type. Many of the modes can be changed with both a manipulator and a member function. Which one you use depends on how convenient it might be for the display at hand. Some of the mode changes remain in place until you change them again. Others reset themselves to their default values after every output message.

Input/Output Member Functions

There are several member functions associated with the **ostream** and **istream** classes that perform input and output. These member functions are alternatives to the extraction and insertion operators providing better ways to manage certain kinds of input and output.

Output Member Functions

put

The **put** member function writes a single character to the output stream. The following two statements are the same:

```
cout.put('A');
cout << 'A';
```

write

The **write** member function writes any block of memory to the stream in binary format. Because **write** does not terminate when it sees a null it is useful for writing the binary representations of data structures to stream files, which are discussed later. Exercise 10.10 illustrates the **write** function with the **cout** object.

```
#include <iostream.h>

main()
{
    static struct    {
        char msg[23];
        int alarm;
        int eol;
    } data = { "It's Howdy Doody time!", '\a', '\n' };

    cout.write( (char *) &data, sizeof data);
}
```

*Exercise 10.10 The **ostream write** Function.*

The message is displayed in Exercise 10.10. The program writes the message, sounds the alarm, and advances to the next line.

Note the cast to **char*** before the address of the structure object. The **write** function accepts **char** pointers and **unsigned char** pointers only. The address of the structure must be cast to one of these.

Input Member Functions

The >> extraction operator has a limitation that programs sometimes need to overcome: the extraction operator bypasses white space. If you type characters on a line that is being read by the extraction operator, only the nonspace characters come into the receiving character variable. The spaces are skipped. Likewise, if the program uses the extraction operator to read a string of words, the input stops when it finds a space character. The next word is read into the next (if any) use of the extraction operation on the **istream** object, and all spaces between the words are lost.

The **istream** class includes the **get** and **getline** member functions to handle reading input characters that must include white space.

get

The **get** member function works just like the >> extraction operator except that white space characters are included in the input.

Exercise 10.11 demonstrates the difference between the two operations.

```
#include <iostream.h>

main()
{
    char line[25], ch = 0, *cp;

    cout << " Type a line terminated by 'x'\n>";
    cp = line;
    while (ch != 'x')      {
```

*Exercise 10.11 The **istream get** Member Function.*

```
        cin >> ch;
        *cp++ = ch;
    }
    *cp = '\0';
    cout << ' ' << line;

    cout << "\n Type another one\n>";
    cp = line;
    ch = 0;
    while (ch != 'x')      {
        cin.get(ch);
        *cp++ = ch;
    }
    *cp = '\0';
    cout << ' ' << line;
}
```

*Exercise 10.11 The **istream get** Member Function (continued).*

In Exercise 10.11, two strings are read from the keyboard one character at a time. The first input uses the extraction operator and the second one uses the **get** member function. If you typed "now is the timex" for both entries, the screen would look like the following display:

```
Type a line terminated by 'x'
now is the timex                (entered by you)
nowisthetimex                   (echoed by the program)
Type another one
now is the timex                (entered by you)
now is the timex                (echoed by the program)
```

You can see that the extraction operator skips over the white space and the **get** function does not. The program needs the **x** terminator because it needs to know when to stop reading. Because **cin** is a buffered object, the program does not begin to start seeing characters until you type the carriage return, and that character is not seen by the program.

A variation of the **get** function allows a program to specify a buffer address and the maximum characters to read.

Exercise 10.12 shows how the **get** function can specify a buffer address and length, instead of a character variable to receive the input.

```
#include <iostream.h>

main()
{
    char line[25];
    cout << " Type a line terminated by carriage return\n>";
    cin.get(line, 25);
    cout << ' ' << line;
}
```

*Exercise 10.12 Using **get** with a Buffer and Length.*

Exercise 10.12 reads whatever you type into the structure and echoes it to the screen.

The length value minus one is the maximum characters that are read into the buffer. You can type more than that number but the excess characters are discarded.

getline

The **getline** function works the same as the variation of the **get** function demonstrated in Exercise 10.12. Both functions allow a third argument that specifies the terminating character for input. If you do not include that argument, its default value is the newline character.

Exercise 10.13 uses the **getline** function with a third argument to specify a terminating character for the input stream.

```
#include <iostream.h>

main()
{
    char line[25];
    cout << " Type a line terminated by 'q'\n>";
    cin.getline(line, 25, 'q');
    cout << ' ' << line;
}
```

*Exercise 10.13 The **istream getline** Member Function.*

If you type "after this I quit," the program screen looks like the following:

```
Type a line terminated by 'q'
after this I quit            (entered by you)
after this I                 (echoed by the program)
```

Note that the Zortech C++ 3.1 compiler includes the terminating character in the final string as shown here:

```
after this I q               (echoed by the program)
```

read

The **istream** class's **read** member function is the input equivalent of the **write** function. It reads the binary representation of the input data into the buffer without bypassing white space. It is usually used with file input/output described later.

Exercise 10.14 is an example of using the **read** function to read a string of characters from the keyboard into a structure.

```
#include <iostream.h>

main()
{
    struct    {
        char msg[23];
    } data;

    cin.read( (char *) &data, sizeof data);
    cout << data.msg;
}
```

*Exercise 10.14 The **istream read** Function.*

Exercise 10.14 reads whatever you type into the structure and echoes it to the screen.

Overloading the << Insertion and >> Extraction Operators

The overloaded insertion and extraction operators work with the standard C++ data types. A user-defined class can overload them to work with the data formats of the class itself making a program more readable. It is clearer when a program can use the second of the following two statements:

```
dt.display(); // call a member function to display
cout << dt;   // send the dt object to the cout object
```

The second statement is also more flexible as you will soon see. The overloaded insertion operator can work with **ostream** objects other than just **cout**. Similarly, the overloaded extraction operator can work with **istream** objects other than just **cin**. You might, for example, display a class on the **cerr** stream or write it to a file.

Overloading <<

Consider the **Date** class that the exercises in this book have used extensively. Usually the **Date** class in an exercise also has a **display** member function that sends the data members to the **cout** object in a date format. The following is a more intuitive way to display a class object:

```
Date dt(1,2,88);
cout << dt;
```

To get the **cout** object to accept a **Date** object along with the insertion operator, the program must overload the insertion operator to recognize an **ostream** object on the left and a **Date** on the right. The overloaded << operator function must then be a friend to the **Date** class definition so that it can access the private data members of the **Date**.

Exercise 10.15 overloads the << insertion operator with an **iostream** object on the left and a **Date** object on the right.

```
#include <iostream.h>

class Date {
    int mo, da, yr;
public:
    Date(int m, int d, int y) { mo = m; da = d; yr = y; }
    friend ostream& operator<< (ostream& os, Date& dt);
};

ostream& operator<< (ostream& os, Date& dt)
{
    os << dt.mo << '/' << dt.da << '/' << dt.yr;
    return os;
}
```

Exercise 10.15 Overloading the << Operator.

```
main()
{
    Date dt(5, 6, 77);
    cout << dt;
}
```

Exercise 10.15 Overloading the << Operator (continued).

Exercise 10.15 displays the date 5/6/77 on the screen.

Overloading >>

Overloading the >> extraction operator allows a class to have an intelligent class input function that knows about the input requirements of the class's data members. Exercise 10.16 is an example of overloading the extraction operator to read a date into the **Date** class.

```
#include <iostream.h>

class Date {
    int mo, da, yr;
public:
    Date() {}
    friend ostream& operator<< (ostream& os, Date& dt);
    friend istream& operator>> (istream& is, Date& dt);
};

ostream& operator<< (ostream& os, Date& dt)
{
    os << dt.mo << '/' << dt.da << '/' << dt.yr;
```

Exercise 10.16 Overloading the >> Operator.

```
      return os;
}

istream& operator>> (istream& is, Date& dt)
{
    is >> dt.mo >> dt.da >> dt.yr;
    return is;
}

main()
{
    Date dt;
    cout << "Enter a date (mm dd yy): ";
    cin >> dt;
    cout << dt;
}
```

Exercise 10.16 Overloading the >> Operator (continued).

Exercise 10.16 displays a date that you enter as shown here:

```
Enter a date (mm dd yy): 6 29 90
6/29/90
```

With the overloaded >> operator in the exercise, the user enters the three components of a date with intervening spaces. The overloaded >> operator in **istream** skips white space, so the **Date** overloaded >> operator function uses that feature to collect three integers from **cin**. You might prefer to read the date into a string with intervening slashes or dashes and then use the C **atoi** function to parse the values into the **Date** class data members. A complete date input function would validate the values for the month, day, and year.

File Input/Output

A file stream is an extension of a console stream. File stream classes are derived from the console stream classes and inherit all of the characteristics of the console. But files have some requirements of their own that character devices such as the console do not have. Files have distinct names. A program can append data to an existing file. A program can seek to a specified position in a file. The class inheritance facility of C++ is a natural way to build file classes from console classes, and that is how the file stream classes work.

A program that uses the file stream classes must include the *fstream.h* header file where the classes are defined. The program might also include *iostream.h*, but it is not necessary because *fstream.h* itself includes *iostream.h*.

The *ofstream* Class

The **ofstream** class objects are files that a program can write to. In the most elementary use of **ofstream**, the program declares an object of type **ofstream**, gives it a name, and writes to it. When the object goes out of scope, the file closes.

Exercise 10.17 uses an **ofstream** object in its simplest form.

```
#include <fstream.h>

main()
{
    ofstream tfile("test.dat");
    tfile << "This is test data";
}
```

Exercise 10.17 File Output.

The program creates a file and writes a string to it.

You can use the **ofstream** class to append to an existing file. Exercise 10.18 appends a string to the file that Exercise 10.17 created.

```
#include <fstream.h>

main()
{
    ofstream tfile("test.dat", ios::app);
    tfile << ", and this is more";
}
```

Exercise 10.18 Appending to an Output File.

The **write** member function works well with **ofstream** classes.

NOTE

The Zortech C++ 3.1 compiler does not implement the **ios::app flag** correctly, and the string is not appended to the file in the exercise.

Exercise 10.19 shows how the **write** function can record the binary representation of a class object into a data file.

```
#include <fstream.h>

class Date    {
    int mo, da, yr;
public:
    Date(int m, int d, int y)
        { mo = m; da = d; yr = y; }
};

main()
{
    Date dt(6, 24, 40);
    ofstream tfile("date.dat");
    tfile.write((char *) &dt, sizeof dt);
}
```

*Exercise 10.19 The **write** Member Function.*

The program creates the file and writes the binary value of the **Date** object into it. The **write** function does not stop writing when it reaches a null character, so the complete class structure is written regardless of its content.

The *ifstream* Class

The **ifstream** class objects are input files. A program can declare an input file stream object and read it. A program can use the >> extraction operator, the **get** function, or the **getline** function just as if the stream were the console device rather than a file. A program can also use the **read** member function to read binary blocks into memory.

Exercise 10.20 is a program that reads the **Date** object from the file written by Exercise 10.19.

```cpp
#include <fstream.h>

class Date     {
    int mo, da, yr;
public:
    Date() { }
    friend ostream& operator<< (ostream& os, Date& dt);
};

ostream& operator<< (ostream& os, Date& dt)
{
    os << dt.mo << '/' << dt.da << '/' << dt.yr;
    return os;
}

main()
{
```

*Exercise 10.20 The **read** Member Function.*

```
    Date dt;
    ifstream tfile("date.dat");
    tfile.read((char *) &dt, sizeof dt);
    cout << dt;
}
```

*Exercise 10.20 The **read** Member Function (continued).*

Exercise 10.20 displays the date 6/24/40 on the screen.

Streams have a number of status bits that reflect the current state of the stream. The values of the bits are defined in an **enum** in the **ios** class, and there are member functions that can test and change the bits. The **eof** member function returns a true value if the stream has reached the end of its character stream.

Exercise 10.21 reads a text file a character at a time, sending each character to **cout** and stopping at end-of-file.

```
#include <fstream.h>

main()
{
    ifstream tfile("test.dat");
    while (!tfile.eof())    {
        char ch;
        tfile.get(ch);
        cout << ch;
    }
}
```

Exercise 10.21 Testing End-of-File.

Exercise 10.21 displays this message:

```
This is test data, and this is more
```

Seeking

Disk drives are random access devices. A program can modify the current position of a file stream by using one of the member functions **seekg** and **seekp**. The **seekg** function changes the position of the next input operation. The **seekp** function changes the position of the next output operation.

Exercise 10.22 opens a file, changes the input position, and then reads to end of file.

```
#include <fstream.h>

main()
{
    ifstream tfile("test.dat");
    tfile.seekg(5);        // seek five characters in
    while (!tfile.eof())    {
        char ch;
        tfile.get(ch);
        cout << ch;
    }
}
```

*Exercise 10.22 The **seekg** Member Function.*

Exercise 10.22 displays this message:

```
is test data, and this is more
```

A program can specify that a **seekg** or **seekp** operation occur relative to the beginning of the file, the end of the file, or the current position by adding an argument to the function call. The argument is defined in an **enum** in the **ios** class. The following are examples of the function calls:

```
tfile.seekg(5, ios::beg);
tfile.seekg(10, ios::cur);
tfile.seekg(-15, ios::end);
```

If you do not provide the second argument, the seek occurs from the beginning of the file.

You can determine the current position for input with the **tellg** member function and the current position for output with the **tellp** member function.

Exercise 10.23 illustrates the **tellg** function.

```
#include <fstream.h>

main()
{
    ifstream tfile("test.dat");
    while (!tfile.eof())     {
        char ch;
        streampos here = tfile.tellg();
        tfile.get(ch);
        if (ch == ' ')
            cout << "\nPosition " << here << " is a space";
    }
}
```

*Exercise 10.23 The **tellg** Function*

Exercise 10.23 displays these messages.

```
Position 4 is a space
Position 7 is a space
Position 12 is a space
Position 18 is a space
Position 22 is a space
```

```
Position 27 is a space
Position 30 is a space
```

The program reads the file built by earlier exercises and displays messages showing the character positions where it finds spaces. The **tellg** function returns an integral value of type **streampos**, a **typedef** defined in *iostream.h*.

The *fstream* Class

The **fstream** class supports file stream objects that a program opens for both input and output. Typical examples are data base files where a program reads records, updates them, and writes them back to the file.

An object of type **fstream** is a single stream with two logical substreams, one for input and one for output. Each of the two substreams has its own position pointer. The pointers follow each other. There are two pointers because they are defined in the **ifstream** and **ofstream** classes and are available to objects of those classes as well.

Files opened in append mode always write to the end of the file. They also change the input position pointer to just past the last character after every write.

Exercise 10.24 is a program that reads the text file from the earlier exercises into a character array and writes an uppercase only copy of the bytes at the end of the file.

```
#include <fstream.h>
#include <ctype.h>

main()
{
    char *fname = "test.dat";
    // --- read the file into an array
    fstream tfile(fname, ios::in);
    char tdata[100];
```

*Exercise 10.24 An **fstream** File.*

```
    int i = 0;
    while (!tfile.eof())
        tfile.get(tdata[i++]);
    tfile.close();
    // --- append the u/c to the file
    tfile.open(fname, ios::app);
    for (int j = 0; j < i-1; j++)
        tfile.put((char)toupper(tdata[j]));
    tfile.close();
}
```

*Exercise 10.24 An **fstream** File (continued).*

The Zortech C++ 3.1 compiler does not implement the **ios::app** flag correctly, and the upper case string is not appended to the file in the exercise.

Opening and Closing a Stream File

A program can declare an **ifstream**, **ofstream**, or **fstream** object without a name. When it does, the object exists, but no file is associated with it. You must then use the **open** member function to associate a file with the **fstream** object. You can disassociate the file from the object by calling the **close** member function. This technique allows a single object to represent different files at different times.

Exercise 10.25 demonstrates the use of the **open** function to associate the stream object with a file and the **close** function to disassociate the object from a file.

```
#include <fstream.h>

main()
{
    ofstream tfile;    // an ofstream object without a file
    tfile.open("test1.dat");
    tfile << "This is TEST1";
    tfile.close();
    tfile.open("test2.dat");
    tfile << "This is TEST2";
    tfile.close();
}
```

Exercise 10.25 ***open*** *and* ***close*** *Member Functions.*

The **iostream** classes include conversion functions that return true or false values if you use the object name in a true/false conditional expression. Suppose you declare a file stream object without an initializing name and do not associate a name with that object. The following code shows how you might test for that condition:

```
fstream tfile;    // no file name given
if (tfile)        // this test returns false
    // ...
```

How to Open a File

The C and C++ stream facilities for opening files are less than instantly intuitive. Veteran programmers still have to stop and think when they are about to open a file. Does the file already exist? May the file already exist? If the file already exists should the program truncate it? Append to it? If the file does not exist should the program create it? The variations on this theme go on and on.

The **open** member function and the implied open operation performed by the constructor take an **open_mode** integer value as a parameter. The argument

values for the **open_mode** parameter are defined in the **ios** class. You option-
ally provide one or more of these parameters in a logical OR expression
depending on how you want the file to be opened.

Following is a list of the **open_mode** bits defined in the **ios** class.

ios::app	Append to an output file. Every output operation is performed at the physical end of file, and the input and output file pointers are repositioned immediately past the last character written.
ios::ate	The **open** operation includes a seek to the end of the file. This mode can be used with input and output files.
ios::in	This is an input file and is an implied mode for **ifstream** objects. If you use **ios::in** as an **open_mode** for an **ofstream** file, it prevents the truncation of an existing file.
ios::out	This is an output file and is an implied mode for **ofstream** objects. When you use **ios::out** for an **ofstream** object without **ios::app** or **ios::ate**, **ios::trunc** is implied.
ios::nocreate	The file must exist, otherwise the **open** fails.
ios::noreplace	The file must not exist, otherwise the **open** fails.
ios::trunc	Delete the file if it already exists and re-create it.

There are seven of these bits. There are three types of objects: **ofstream**,
ifstream, and **fstream**. Therefore, there are 381 possible open statements for
you to code. Not all of them would be logical, but you could code them all. For
each of them, the file might exist or it might not. Therefore, there are 762 possible circumstances. Covering them all is beyond the scope of this book.
However, here are some of the most common circumstances:

1. You want to create a file. If it exists, delete the old one.

    ```
    ofstream ofile("FILENAME");  // no open_mode
    ```

2. You want to read an existing file. If it does not exist, an error has occurred.

    ```
    ifstream ifile("FILENAME");  // no open_mode
    if (ifile.fail())
        // the file does not exist ...
    ```

3. You want to read and write an existing file. This is an update mode. You might read records, seek to records, rewrite existing records, and add records to the end of the file.

```
fstream ffile("FILENAME", ios::in | ios::out | ios::nocreate);
if (ffile.fail())
    // the file does not exist ...
```

4. You want to write to an existing file without deleting it first.

```
ofstream ofile("FILENAME", ios::in);
```

5. You want to append records to an existing file, creating it if it does not exist.

```
ofstream ofile("FILENAME", ios::out | ios::app);
```

Testing Errors

A program can and should test errors when it uses input/output file streams. Each stream object has its own set of condition flags that change according to the current state of the object. You already used one of these flags when you tested for end-of-file with the **eof** member function. Other member functions that test for flag settings are **bad**, **fail**, and **good**. The **bad** function returns a true value if your program attempts to do something illegal such as seek beyond the end of the file. The **fail** function returns a true value for all conditions that include the **bad** positive return plus any valid operations that fail such as trying to open an unavailable file or trying to write to a disk device that is full. The **good** function returns true whenever **fail** would return false.

Exercise 10.26 attempts and fails to open a nonexisting file for input.

```
#include <fstream.h>

main()
{
    ifstream ifile;
    ifile.open("noname.fil", ios::in | ios::nocreate);
    if (ifile.fail())
        cout << "Cannot open";
    else    {
        // ...
        ifile.close();
    }
}
```

Exercise 10.26 File Error Checking.

Exercise 10.26 displays the "Cannot open" message on the screen.

Note the use of the **ios::nocreate** mode value as an argument to the **open** member function. This argument tells the **open** function to **fail** if the file does not exist. Therefore, the call to the fail member function returns true because the file does not exist. This function works the same way whether you open the file with the **open** member function or specify the file name as an initializer in the declaration of the stream object.

Summary

The C++ Stream Library has many other features and facilities. For example, there is a set of classes that supports in-memory formatting much like the **sprintf** and **sscanf** functions of C but with all of the insertion and extraction operations and member functions of the **iostream** classes.

With the introduction in this chapter you have learned how to use C++ stream classes as they apply to most input/output applications. After you have used them for a while you might want to read the description of their advanced features in the documentation that accompanies your compiler.

Templates

C++ version 3.0 added the *template* to the language, a feature that had been only experimental in earlier versions. This chapter shows you how and when to use templates. You will learn:

- Class templates
- Function templates

The functions in this chapter compile only with compilers that have implemented templates. The Microsoft 8.0 compiler has not implemented them, although Microsoft promises to have the feature in their C++ package soon.

Class Templates

Class templates, sometimes called *parameterized* data types, allow you to describe a generic data type to manage other data types. Class templates are typically used to build general-purpose container classes, such as stacks, lists, and queues, where the maintenance of the container is generic but the item in the container is specific.

Consider the **ListEntry** linked list class that you used in Exercises 7.20 and 7.24. These particular linked list classes manage lists of character pointers. A program might need several linked lists, with each one managing a different data type.

By using a class template, you can define a generic linked-list class with an unspecified data type to be in the list. Then you can define associate specific classes with the template.

The format of a class template specification is shown in this example:

```
template<class T>
class LinkedList {
    T& p;
    // ...
public:
    // ...
    void AddEntry(T &entry);
};
```

The template specifies objects of type **LinkedList** with an unspecified data type as a parameter. Users of the template specify the data type to be managed by the list.

The first part of a class template definition and its member function definitions is the template specifier as shown here:

```
template<class T>
```

The **T** identifier represents the parameterized data type throughout the definition. The identifier can be any C++ data type including intrinsic types and classes. The use of **T** for the primary template parameter is a convention, although you can use any valid C++ identifier.

You must provide template functions for the member functions of a parameterized data type. The **LinkedList** example has an **AddEntry** member function. You define the function as shown here:

```
template<class T>
void LinkedList<T>::AddEntry(T &entry)
{
    // ...
}
```

These function definitions are in the header file that contains the class definition. They must be visible to the program that declares objects of the class template. They do not generate any code until they are used.

You declare an object of a class template by specifying the name of the class and the data type for which it will operate like this:

```
LinkedList<int> IntList;
```

This statement declares an object from the **LinkedList** template with the **int** data type as the parameter.

Think of templates as macros. The compiler uses the object declaration to build the class definition and functions. The compiler substitutes the template argument, **int** in the example just shown, for the template parameter, **T** in the **LinkedList** template example.

You can declare more than one object of a class template in the same program. For example, given the **LinkedList** template just shown, a program can declare two different linked lists, as shown here:

```
LinkedList<char *> StrList;
LinkedList<Date> DateList;
```

These statements declare two **LinkedList** objects. The first one is a list of character pointers. The second one is a list of **Date** objects. These two statements cause the compiler to generate two copies of all of the member functions in the template. Each copy is customized to work with the type specified in the declaration. In this example, there is a copy of the code for character pointers and one for the **Date** class. Wherever the template definition uses **T**, the compiler will substitute **char*** for the first object and **Date** for the second. That means that the code in the template's member functions must work in the context of those types.

If you use the same data types for two different objects of the same template, as shown next, the compiler generates only one set of code for the two objects.

```
LinkedList<int> monthList;
LinkedList<int> yearList;
```

The using program calls the template functions just as it calls member functions of other classes. For example, you can add entries to the **LinkedList** objects with these calls:

```
Date dt(6,24,93);        // a date
DateList.AddEntry(dt);   // add the date to DateList

char *name = "Dolly";    // a string
StrList.AddEntry(name);  // add the string to StrList

int n = 123;             // an int
IntList.AddEntry(n);     // add the int to IntList
```

A template can contain more than one data type parameter, making it possible to build parameterized data types of considerable complexity. The parameters can be generic classes, which are identified by the class keyword. Other parameters may be specific data types as shown here:

```
template <class T, class S, int b>
```

At least one parameter should be a generic class. Otherwise the definition would define the usual data type rather than a parameterized one. When you declare an object of the class template, you must use actual types where they are called for. In the example just shown, you can use any type for the first two parameters, but the third type must be an **int**.

Exercise 11.1 illustrates how a class template works.

```
#include <iostream.h>

template<class T1, class T2>
class MyTemp {
    T1 t1;
    T2 t2;
public:
    MyTemp(T1 tt1, T2 tt2)
        { t1 = tt1; t2 = tt2; }
    void display()
        { cout << t1 << ' ' << t2 << '\n'; }
};

main()
{
    int a = 123;
    double b = 456.789;
    MyTemp<int, double> mt(a, b);
    mt.display();
}
```

Exercise 11.1 A Simple Template Class.

The template in Exercise 11.1 builds a parameterized type from two parameters. The class template only stores and displays values. The main function declares an object of the type with an **int** and a **double** as the parameters. Then it tells the object to display itself. Exercise 11.1 displays this output:

```
123 456.789
```

The template in Exercise 11.1 points out something to consider when you use a template. The template sends its parameterized types to the **cout** object by using the << insertion operator. Therefore, any type that you use with the template must be compatible with that operation. Exercise 11.1 works because **iostreams** can accept **ints** and **doubles** with the << operator. As you will see later, the same must be true of any other type. If the template uses relational operators to compare objects of the parameterized type, then the type must be able to use those operators, too. The intrinsic types will work fine, but your user-defined types will not if you have not overloaded the relational operators.

A Bounded Array Class Template

C and C++ programmers often build bugs into their programs because the language does not test that an array subscript is within the bounds of the array. The following code passes the compiler's error tests and executes with no run-time bounds checking.

```
main()
{
    int array[10];
    for (int i = 0; i <= 10; i++)
        array[i] = 123;
}
```

The problem with the code is that the subscript is allowed to go beyond the end of the array. The array has 10 elements. The subscript is allowed to go as high as 10, which references the eleventh element, which does not exist. However, the program will write an integer in the next integer position in memory beyond the array. The result depends on the program and the compiler. If you are lucky, the program will abort early in testing and you will find the problem. If you are not so lucky, the eleventh array element will be in some usually harmless position, and you will not encounter the bug until much later when it is more difficult to isolate.

Other languages have bounded arrays. The run-time system does not allow you to address an array with a subscript that is beyond its limits. The cost is in run-time efficiency.

You can use the template to add bounded arrays to your programs without adding a lot of overhead. The technique depends on your understanding of not only templates, but the Standard C **assert** macro as well. Immediately following is **barray.h**, the class template for the bounded array.

```
// ------ barray.h

#ifndef BARRAY_H
#define BARRAY_H

#include <assert.h>

// --- a bounded array template
template <class T, int b>
class Array     {
    T elem [b];
public:
    T& operator[] (int sub)
    {
        assert(sub >= 0 && sub < b);
        return elem[sub];
    }
};

#endif
```

This simple template has one purpose, to check all subscripted references to array elements and abort the program if a subscript is out of bounds. Observe that the template specifier has two parameter types:

```
template <class T, int b>
```

If the template included **non-inline** member functions, this statement would be immediately ahead of the function definition as well.

The overloaded subscript operator **([ ])** function in the **Array** class template grants read-write subscripted access to elements of the array. The **assert** macro validates the subscript's value. If the value is less than zero or greater than the array's dimension minus one, the **assert** macro displays an error message on the stderr device and aborts the program.

Exercise 11.2 is a program that uses the bounded array template.

```cpp
#include <iostream.h>
#include <iomanip.h>
#include "barray.h"
#include "date.h"

main()
{
    // ---- a bounded array of dates
    Array<Date, 5> dateArray;

    // ----- some dates
    Date dt1(12,17,37);
    Date dt2(11,30,38);
    Date dt3(6,24,40);
    Date dt4(10,31,42);
    Date dt5(8,5,44);

    // ----- put the dates in the array
    dateArray[0] = dt1;
    dateArray[1] = dt2;
    dateArray[2] = dt3;
    dateArray[3] = dt4;
    dateArray[4] = dt5;
```

Exercise 11.2 Using a Bounded Array Template.

```
    // ------ display the dates
    for (int i = 0; i < 5; i++)    {
        dateArray[i].display();
        cout << '\n';
    }
    cout << flush;
    // ---- try to put a date in the array
    //      outside the range of the subscript
    Date dt6(1,29,92);
    dateArray[5] = dt6;  // template's assertion aborts
}
```

Exercise 11.2 Using a Bounded Array Template (continued).

Make sure that you link this program with the *date.cpp* program from Chapter 9.
The program declares an **Array** object of **Date** objects with a subscript limit of
five. Then it declares five **Date** objects, which it puts into the array. After displaying all five objects, the program flushes **cout** and then tries to put another
Date object into the array's sixth position, which does not exist. The **assert**
macro's test is false, and the program aborts. Exercise 11.2 displays this output:

```
12/17/37
11/30/38
6/24/40
10/31/42
8/5/44
Assertion failed: sub >= 0 && sub < b,
file barray.h, line 11
Abnormal program termination
```

The format of the **error** message depends on the compiler, but the information
displayed is the same.

After your program is fully tested, you can remove the assertion code by inserting this line before the inclusion of **assert.h**:

```
#define NDEBUG
```

When to Use Class Templates

Templates surround other types with generic management. The types that you provide as parameters have their own behavior. The class templates provide a way to contain objects of those classes in general purpose containers. The details of their containment are unrelated to their purposes. A **Date** class has its own behavior. So does a **String** class. So does a class that encapsulates a person's name, address, and phone number. Their participation in a queue, list, bag, linked list, balanced tree, or any other kind of container is unrelated to their purpose. It is natural and proper to use the features of a programming language to separate these two unrelated behaviors.

Before C++ supported templates programmers used inheritance to associate a data type with a container class. In other cases they would build cumbersome classes that used void pointers and casts to manage the containment of unrelated types in various containers. These approaches worked well enough, but they are not always the best ones. As a general rule, you should use inheritance when the derived class modifies the functional behavior of the base. When the relationship manages objects of the class without changing the class's behavior, you should use templates.

There are other considerations, however. If the management algorithm entails a lot of code in the class definition and its member functions, you should think twice before you build the algorithm as a template. Remember that each distinct use of the template generates a new copy of the code. If the template manages a significant number of different types, the executable program can be big.

A Linked List Template

You used the **LinkedList** class at the beginning of this chapter to see how templates work. Now you will implement a complete **LinkedList** class template. Immediately following is *linklist.h*, the header file that defines the **LinkedList** template.

```
// ----------- linklist.h
// a template for a linked list

#ifndef LINKLIST_H
#define LINKLIST_H

template <class T> class LinkedList;

template <class T>
// --- the linked list entry
class ListEntry    {
    T thisentry;
    ListEntry *nextentry;
    ListEntry *preventry;
    ListEntry(T& entry);
    friend class LinkedList<T>;
};

template <class T>
// ---- construct a linked list entry
ListEntry<T>::ListEntry(T &entry)
{
    thisentry = entry;
    nextentry = 0;
    preventry = 0;
}

template <class T>
// ---- the linked list
class LinkedList    {
    // --- the listhead
```

(continued)

```cpp
    ListEntry<T> *firstentry;
    ListEntry<T> *lastentry;
    ListEntry<T> *iterator;
    void RemoveEntry(ListEntry<T> *lentry);
    void InsertEntry(T& entry, ListEntry<T> *lentry);
public:
    LinkedList();
    ~LinkedList();
    void AppendEntry(T& entry);
    void RemoveEntry(int pos = -1);
    void InsertEntry(T&entry, int pos = -1);
    T *FindEntry(int pos);
    T *CurrentEntry();
    T *FirstEntry();
    T *LastEntry();
    T *NextEntry();
    T *PrevEntry();
};

template <class T>
// ---- construct a linked list
LinkedList<T>::LinkedList()
{
    iterator = 0;
    firstentry = 0;
    lastentry = 0;
}

template <class T>
// ---- destroy a linked list
```

(continued)

```
LinkedList<T>::~LinkedList()
{
    while (firstentry)
        RemoveEntry(firstentry);
}

template <class T>
// ---- append an entry to the linked list
void LinkedList<T>::AppendEntry(T& entry)
{
    ListEntry<T> *newentry = new ListEntry<T>(entry);
    newentry->preventry = lastentry;
    if (lastentry)
        lastentry->nextentry = newentry;
    if (firstentry == 0)
        firstentry = newentry;
    lastentry = newentry;
}

template <class T>
// ---- remove an entry from the linked list
void LinkedList<T>::RemoveEntry(ListEntry<T> *lentry)
{
    if (lentry == 0)
        return;
    if (lentry == iterator)
        iterator = lentry->preventry;
    // ---- repair any break made by this removal
    if (lentry->nextentry)
        lentry->nextentry->preventry = lentry->preventry;
```

(continued)

```cpp
        if (lentry->preventry)
            lentry->preventry->nextentry = lentry->nextentry;
        // --- maintain listhead if this is last and/or first
        if (lentry == lastentry)
            lastentry = lentry->preventry;
        if (lentry == firstentry)
            firstentry = lentry->nextentry;
        delete lentry;
}

template <class T>
// ---- insert an entry into the linked list
void LinkedList<T>::InsertEntry(T& entry, ListEntry<T>
*lentry)
{
    ListEntry<T> *newentry = new ListEntry<T>(entry);
    newentry->nextentry = lentry;
    if (lentry)    {
        newentry->preventry = lentry->preventry;
        lentry->preventry = newentry;
    }
    if (newentry->preventry)
        newentry->preventry->nextentry = newentry;
    if (lentry == firstentry)
        firstentry = newentry;
}

template <class T>
// ---- remove an entry from the linked list
void LinkedList<T>::RemoveEntry(int pos)
{
```

(continued)

```
        FindEntry(pos);
        RemoveEntry(iterator);
    }

    template <class T>
    // ---- insert an entry into the linked list
    void LinkedList<T>::InsertEntry(T& entry, int pos)
    {
        FindEntry(pos);
        InsertEntry(entry, iterator);
    }

    template <class T>
    // ---- return the current linked list entry
    T *LinkedList<T>::CurrentEntry()
    {
        return iterator ? &(iterator->thisentry) : 0;
    }

    template <class T>
    // ---- return a specific linked list entry
    T *LinkedList<T>::FindEntry(int pos)
    {
        if (pos != -1)    {
            iterator = firstentry;
            if (iterator)    {
                while (pos--)
                    iterator = iterator->nextentry;
            }
        }
```

(continued)

```
        return CurrentEntry();
    }

    template <class T>
    // ---- return the first entry in the linked list
    T *LinkedList<T>::FirstEntry()
    {
        iterator = firstentry;
        return CurrentEntry();
    }

    template <class T>
    // ---- return the last entry in the linked list
    T *LinkedList<T>::LastEntry()
    {
        iterator = lastentry;
        return CurrentEntry();
    }

    template <class T>
    // ---- return the next entry in the linked list
    T *LinkedList<T>::NextEntry()
    {
        if (iterator == 0)
            iterator = firstentry;
        else
            iterator = iterator->nextentry;
        return CurrentEntry();
    }
```

(continued)

```
template <class T>
// ---- return the previous entry in the linked list
T *LinkedList<T>::PrevEntry()
{
    if (iterator == 0)
        iterator = lastentry;
    else
        iterator = iterator->preventry;
    return CurrentEntry();
}

#endif
```

This template definition builds a linked list of objects of any type. After the list is built, the user can navigate it by using the template's member functions, which return pointers to the objects in the list.

There are two templates in the **linklist.h** file. The first one is for the **ListEntry** class, which the **LinkedList** class uses. A using program cannot declare an object of this class. Observe that there is no public constructor. Only a **friend** of this class template can use it; the **LinkedList** class is a **friend**. The Listentry class contains the object that will be in the list and pointers to the next and previous objects in the list.

The **LinkedList** template contains what is called the **listhead**, a data structure that includes pointers to the first and last entry in the class and an **iterator** pointer that the class uses to navigate the list. These pointers point to **ListEntry** objects.

There are two **private** member functions for the **LinkedList** class to use to insert and remove **ListEntry** objects from the list. The **LinkedList** class constructs and destroys these **ListEntry** objects.

The **LinkedList** class's public interface consists of a constructor and destructor, member functions to let the user append, insert, and remove objects of the type, and member functions to let the user navigate the list. The following exercises demonstrate this behavior.

A Linked List of Integers

Exercise 11.3 is a program that uses the **LinkedList** class to maintain a list of integers.

```cpp
#include <iostream.h>
#include "linklist.h"

main()
{
    LinkedList<int> IntList;
    // --- add 10 integers to the linked list
    for (int i = 0; i < 10; i++)
        IntList.AppendEntry(i);
    // --- iterate thru the 10 and remove #5
    int *ip = IntList.FirstEntry();
    while (ip)    {
        cout << *ip << ' ';
        if (*ip == 5)
            IntList.RemoveEntry();
        ip = IntList.NextEntry();
    }
    // --- iterate thru what's left
    cout << '\n';
    while ((ip = IntList.NextEntry()) != 0)
        cout << *ip << ' ';
}
```

Exercise 11.3 Using a Linked List Template for Integers .

The program in Exercise 11.3 declares a **LinkedList** object with **int** as the type parameter. Then it adds 10 integers to the list. Next the program uses a **FirstEntry** call and a series of **NextEntry** calls to iterate through the list, displaying each integer as it retrieves it. When it finds the list entry with the value 5, the program calls **RemoveEntry** to remove the entry from the list. When it is at the end, the program iterates through the list a second time, displaying the values to prove that number 5 was removed. Exercise 11.3 displays this output.

```
0 1 2 3 4 5 6 7 8 9
0 1 2 3 4 6 7 8 9
```

A Linked List of Dates

Exercise 11.4 uses the **LinkedList** template to build and maintain a list of **Date** objects. For this exercise you will need to link the program with the **Date** class from Chapter 9.

```cpp
#include <iostream.h>
#include "linklist.h"
#include "date.h"

main()
{
    LinkedList<Date> DateList;
    Date dt1(12,17,37);
    Date dt2(11,30,38);
    Date dt3(6,24,40);
    Date dt4(10,31,42);
    Date dt5(8,5,44);
    // --- add 5 dates to the linked list
    DateList.AppendEntry(dt1);
    DateList.AppendEntry(dt2);
    DateList.AppendEntry(dt3);
    DateList.AppendEntry(dt4);
```

*Exercise 11.4 Using a Linked List Template for **Dates**.*

```
        DateList.AppendEntry(dt5);
        // --- iterate thru the dates
        cout << "---Forward---\n";
        Date *dp;
        while ((dp = DateList.NextEntry()) != 0)    {
            dp->display();
            cout << '\n';
        }
        // --- insert a date
        Date dt6(1,29,92);
        DateList.InsertEntry(dt6, 3);
        // --- iterate thru the dates
        cout << "---Backward---\n";
        dp = DateList.LastEntry();
        while (dp != 0)    {
            dp->display();
            cout << '\n';
            dp = DateList.PrevEntry();
        }
    }
```

*Exercise 11.4 Using a Linked List Template for **Dates** (continued).*

The program in Exercise 11.4 declares a **LinkedList** object with the **Date** type. Then it declares five **Date** objects, which it puts into the list by calling the **AppendEntry** function. The program iterates through the list and displays the date objects. Then it inserts a **Date** by calling the **InsertEntry** function with a **Date** object and the integer parameter 3. The integer parameter specifies that the insertion is to occur before the fourth entry in the list. A zero value would insert the object at the front of the list. Finally, the program iterates through the list in reverse order by calling **LastEntry** and then **PrevEntry** until there are no more entries returned. The exercise displays the dates in reverse order to prove that the insertion worked. Exercise 11.4 displays this output.

```
---Forward---
12/17/37
11/30/38
6/24/40
10/31/42
8/5/44
---Backward---
8/5/44
10/31/42
1/29/92
6/24/40
11/30/38
12/17/37
```

Function Templates

A template can define a parameterized nonmember function. The usual example substitutes templates for the **min** and **max** macros in C. First, however, consider those macros:

```
#define min(a,b) ((a)<(b)?(a):(b))
#define max(a,b) ((a)>(b)?(a):(b))
```

As you learned in Chapter 2, these macros have problems related to side effects. Suppose you call one of the macros this way:

```
a = min(b++, --c);
```

The **min** macro would expand that expression into this:

```
a = (b++) < (--c) ? (b++) : (--c);
```

The side effects occur when either b gets incremented twice or c gets decremented twice depending on which one is greater. C++ overcomes that problem with the **inline** function as shown here.

```
inline int min(int a, int b)
{
    return (a < b ? a : b);
}
```

There are no side effects, but there is a problem. The **min** function now works with integers only. If your type cannot be converted to a meaningful integral value, then it will not work with the **inline min** function. The apparent solution is to use a function template as shown here:

```
template<class T>
T& min(T& a, T& b)
{
    return (a < b ? a : b);
}
```

This solution isn't perfect either. It won't work unless both objects being compared are of the same type. But at least now you have one more choice.

Sorting with a Template

Another popular example for the function template is to use it to sort arrays of parameterized types. The Standard C **qsort** function does that by having you provide a comparing call-back function. With a template, however, the solution is easier. Immediately following is *quiksort.h*, the definition of the **quicksort** function template.

```
// -------- quiksort.h
#ifndef QUIKSORT_H
#define QUIKSORT_H

// ---- template function for quicksort algorithm

template<class T>
void swap(T& t1, T& t2)
{

    T hold = t2;
    t2 = t1;
    t1 = hold;

}

template<class T>
void quicksort(T array[], int n)
{
    if (n > 1)    {
        int j = n;
        // --- approximate median key
        T medKey = array[j/2];
        // --- swap the median key with the first
        swap(array[j/2], array[0]);
        // sort everything higher than median above it
        // and everything lower below it
        for (int i = 0; i < j; )    {
            while (array[++i] < medKey && i < j-1)

                ;
            while (array[--j] > medKey)

                ;
```

(continued)

```
            if (i < j)
                swap(array[j], array[i]);
        }
        array[0] = array[j];
        array[j] = medKey;
        // --- sort the bottom set
        quicksort(array, j);
        // --- sort the top set
        quicksort(array+j+1, n-j-1);
    }
}

#endif
```

The template implements the **quicksort** algorithm. It sorts an array of types. Its parameters are the **address** of the array and the **number** of elements in the array.

The **quicksort** algorithm divides the array into two parts. First it selects an element to represent the median value. Then it places all elements greater than that value in the upper part and all of the lower elements in the lower part. Then it calls itself recursively, once for each of the two parts. When there is only one part left, the array is fully sorted.

 Due to bugs in the Zortech 3.1 compiler implementation of templates, the exercises that use the **quicksort** function template do not work with Zortech.

Exercise 11.5 is a program that uses the **quicksort** function template to sort integers.

```
#include <iostream.h>
#include <iomanip.h>
#include <stdlib.h>
#include "quiksort.h"

main()
{
    int dim;
    // --- get the number of integers to sort
    cout << "How many integers?\n";
    cin >> dim;
    // --- build an array of random integers
    int *arrs = new int[dim];
    for (int i = 0; i < dim; i++)
        arrs[i] = rand();
    // --- display the random integers
    cout << "\n----- unsorted -----\n";
    for (i = 0; i < dim; i++)
        cout << setw(8) << arrs[i];
    // --- sort the arry
    quicksort(arrs, dim);
    // --- display the sorted integers
    cout << "\n----- sorted -----\n";
    for (i = 0; i < dim; i++)
        cout << setw(8) << arrs[i];
    delete arrs;
}
```

*Exercise 11.5 Using the **Quicksort** Function Template.*

The program in Exercise 11.5 builds an array of integers, reading the dimension for the array from the keyboard. It uses the Standard C **rand** function to fill the array with random numbers and displays the numbers in their random sequence. Then it calls the **quicksort** template function to sort the array. Finally, the program displays the array in its new sequence.

Summary

Templates are the major addition that version 3.0 brought to the C++ language. They add what has been called *genericity* to the language, an object-oriented feature the lack of which many programmers saw as a major shortcoming in earlier in versions.

This chapter is the end of the tutorial exercises with which you taught yourself C++. You now know enough about the language to use it in the design and development of some complex and interesting programs. Chapter 12 describes exception handling, a proposed feature that has not yet been released by AT&T or any of the compiler vendors.

Exception Handling

Exception handling is a new C++ feature that lets a program intercept and process exceptional conditions—errors, usually—in an orderly, organized, and consistent manner. Exception handling has not been implemented yet in C++ compilers at the time this book is being written. The AT&T specification is complete and published, the ANSI X3J16 C++ Standards Committee is adopting the specification, and Dr. Stroustrup has implemented exception handling in his laboratory version of CFRONT.

This chapter contains no exercises because there are no compilers with which to develop and test them. Instead, you will find discussion and code examples to read. You will learn about:

- Traditional C exception handling
- Why traditional methods do not work in C++
- The C++ try/throw/catch idiom
- Anomalies in C++ exception handling

Exception handling allows one section of a program to sense and dispatch error conditions and another section to handle them. It is not unusual for one category of code, perhaps the classes and functions in a library, to know how to detect errors without knowing the appropriate handling strategy. It is just as usual for other categories of code to understand how to deal with errors without being able to detect them.

For example, a class library function may perform math, detecting overflow, underflow, divide-by-zero, and other exceptional conditions that are the result of user input. Selection of a strategy for handling the exception depends on the application. Some programs write **error** messages on the console; others display dialog boxes in a graphical user interface; some request the user to enter better data; others terminate the program. The error could result from a bug in the program or an invalid (and unvalidated) user input. A reusable library function should not presume to know the best exception handling strategy for all applications. On the other hand, an application cannot be expected to detect all possible exceptions.

An example of this relationship is the bounded array class template in Chapter 11. The class detects when an array subscript is out of range by using the **assert** macro, which terminates the program. A more appropriate behavior would be to detect and report the error to the class user and let the user determine how to handle it.

This relationship—that a distant function can report an error to the using program—has implications. Somehow, the detecting function must return control to the handling function through an orderly sequence of function returns. The detecting function can be many function calls deep. An orderly return to the higher level of the handler function requires—at the very least—a coordinated unwinding of the stack.

Exception Handling in C

Traditional C programs take two approaches to exception handling: they follow each function call with a test for errors; and they use **setjmp** and **longjmp** to intercept error conditions. The first approach, which uses something like **errno** and NULL or ERROR function return values to report the nature of the error, is reliable but tedious. Programmers tend to avoid or overlook all of the possibilities. The **setjmp/longjmp** approach is closer to what C++ exception handling strives for: an orderly and automatic way to unwind the stack to a state that was recorded at a specified place higher in the function call hierarchy.

The **setjmp/longjmp** approach is intended to intercept and handle conditions that do not require immediate program termination.

Example: A programming language translator's syntax checker can be in the depths of a recursive descent parser when it detects a syntax error. The program does not need to terminate. It should simply report the error and find its way back to where it can read the next statement and continue. The program uses **setjmp** to identify that place and **longjmp** to get back to it. Following is a code fragment that represents that process.

```
#include <setjmp.h>
jmp_buf jb;
void Validate()
{
    int err;
    err = setjmp(jb);
    if (err)
        /* An exception has occurred */
        ReportError(err);
    while (getInput())
        parse();
}
// --- parse a line of input
void parse()
{
    /* parse the input */
    /* ... */
    if (error)
        longjmp(jb, ErrorCode);
}
```

The **longjmp** call unwinds the stack to its state as recorded in the **jmp_buf** by the **setjmp** call. The initial **setjmp** call returns zero. The **longjmp** call jumps to a return from the **setjmp** call and causes **setjmp** to seem to return the specified error code, which should be nonzero.

There are anomalies in this scheme, however. As you will soon learn, C++ exception handling does not solve them, either. Suppose that the **parse** function looked like this:

```
void parse()
{
    FILE *fp = fopen(fname, "rt");
    char *cp = malloc(1000);
    /* parse the input */
    /* ... */
    if (error)
        longjmp(jb, ErrorCode);
    free(cp);
    fclose(fp);
}
```

Ignore for the moment that in a real program the function would test for exceptions to the **fopen** and **malloc** calls. The two calls represent resources that the program acquires before and releases after the **longjmp** call. The calls could be in interim functions that are called after the **setjmp** operation and that themselves called the **parse** function. The point is that the **longjmp** call occurs before those resources are released. Therefore, every exception in this program represents two system resources that are lost—a *heap segment* and a *file handle*. In the case of the FILE * resource, subsequent attempts to open the same file would fail. If each pass through the system opened a different file—a temporary file with a system-generated file name, for example—the program would fail when the operating system ran out of file handles. Programmers traditionally solve this problem by structuring their programs to avoid it. Either they manage and clean up resources before calling **longjmp** or they do not use **longjmp** where there are interim resources at risk. In the function just shown, the problem is solved by moving the **longjmp** call below the free and **fclose** calls. It is not always that simple, however.

Unwinding the stack in a C program involves resetting the **stack** pointer to where it was pointed when **setjmp** was called. The **jmp_buf** stores everything that the program needs to know to do that. This procedure works because the

stack contains automatic variables and function return addresses. Resetting the stack pointer essentially discards the automatic variables and forgets about the function return addresses, all of which is correct behavior, because the automatic variables are no longer needed and the interim functions will not be resumed.

Exception Handling in C++

Using **longjmp** to unwind the stack in a C++ program does not work, because automatic variables on the stack include objects of classes, and those objects need to execute their destructor functions. Consider this modification to the **parse** function, which is now in a C++ program:

```
void parse()
{
    String str("Parsing now");
    // parse the input
    // ...
    if (error)
        longjmp(jb, ErrorCode);
}
```

Assume that the constructor for the **String** class allocates memory for the string value from the heap. Its destructor returns that memory to the heap. In this program, however, the **String** destructor does not execute because **longjmp** unwinds the stack and jumps to the **setjmp** call before the **str String** object goes out of scope. The memory used by the **str** object itself is returned to the stack, but the heap memory pointed to by a pointer in the string is not returned to the heap.

The problem just shown is one that C++ exception handling solves. The unwinding of the stack in the exception handling and **throw** operation—the analogue to **longjmp**—includes calls to the destructors of automatic objects. Furthermore, if the throw occurs from within the constructor of an automatic object, its destructor is not called, although the destructors of objects embedded in the throwing object are called.

The *try* Block

C++ functions that can sense and recover from errors execute from within a **try** block that looks like this:

```
try  {
    // C++ statements
}
```

Code executing outside of any **try** block is not able to detect or handle exceptions. **Try** blocks may be nested. The **try** block typically calls other functions that are able to detect exceptions.

The *catch* Exception Handler

A **try** block is followed by a **catch** exception handler with a parameter list as shown here:

```
try  {
    // C++ statements
}
catch(int err)   {
    // error-handling code
}
```

There can be multiple **catch** handlers with different parameter lists.

```
try  {
    // C++ statements
}
catch(int err)   {
    // error-handling code
}
catch(char *msg)   {
    // error-handling code with char *
}
```

The **catch** handler is identified by the type in its parameter list. The parameter in the **catch** parameter list does not have to be named. If the parameter is named, it declares an object with that name, and the exception detection code can pass a value in the parameter. If the parameter is unnamed, the exception detection code can jump to the **catch** exception handler merely by naming the type.

The *throw* Statement

To detect an exception and jump to a **catch** handler, a C++ function issues the **throw** statement with a data type that matches the parameter list of the proper **catch** handler like this:

```
throw "An error has occurred";
```

This **throw** statement would jump to the **catch** exception handler function that has the **char*** parameter list.

The **throw** statement unwinds the stack, cleaning up all objects declared within the **try** block by calling their destructors. Next, **throw** calls the matching **catch** handler, passing the **parameter** object.

The *try/throw/catch* Sequence

The following code fragment begins to bring it all together:

```
main()
{
    // --- the try block
    try {
        foo(); // call a lower function
    }
    // --- catch exception handler
    catch(int errcode)   {
        // error-handling code
    }
```

(continued)

```
}
// --- program function
void foo()
{
    // C++ statements to do stuff
    if (error)
        throw -1;
}
```

In the example just shown, the program enters a **try** block, which means that functions called directly or indirectly from within the **try** block can **throw** exceptions. In other words, the **foo** function can **throw** exceptions and so can any function called by **foo**, and so on.

The **catch** exception handler function immediately following the **try** block is the only handler in this example. It **catches** exceptions that are **thrown** with an **int** parameter.

Catch handlers and their matching **throw** statements can have a parameter of any type. For example:

```
catch(Date dt) { ... }
// ...
throw Date(da,mo,yr);
```

This example assumes that there is a class named **Date** that can be constructed with the **da**, **mo**, **yr** parameter list. The **throw** statement builds a temporary object of type **Date** and initializes the object with the values given in the **throw** statement. The parameter may be an automatic variable within the block that uses **throw**, even if the **catch** uses a reference, as shown here:

```
void bar()
{
    try {
        foo();
    }
    catch(Date& dt)   {
        // ...
    }
}
// ...
void foo()
{
    // ...
    if (error) {
        Date dt(da,mo,yr);
        throw dt;
    }
}
```

The **throw** statement builds a temporary **Date** object to pass to the **catch** handler. The automatic **Date** object in the **foo** function is allowed to go out of scope. The temporary **Date** object is not destroyed until the **catch** handler completes processing.

When a **try** block has more than one **catch** handler, a **throw** executes the one that matches the parameter list. That handler is the only one to execute unless it **throws** an exception to execute a different **catch** handler. When the executing **catch** handler exits, the program proceeds with the code following the last **catch** handler.

Exception Specification

You can specify the exceptions that a function may **throw** when you declare the function as shown here:

```
void f() throw(char *, int)
{
    // C++ statements
    if (err1)
        throw 123;
    if (err2)
        throw("Error 2");
}
```

Unexpected Exceptions

If a function includes an exception-specification as shown above, and the function **throws** an exception not given in the specification, the exception is passed to a system function named **unexpected()**. The **unexpected** function calls the latest function named as an argument in a call to the **set_unexpected** function, which returns its current setting. A function with no exception specification can **throw** any exception.

Catch-all Exception Handlers

A **catch** handler with ellipses for a parameter list, shown next, catches all exceptions:

```
catch(...)   {
    // error-handling code
}
```

In a group of **catches** associated with a **try** block, the **catch-all** handler must appear last.

Throwing an Exception from a Handler

You can code a **throw** with no operand in a **catch** handler or in a function called by one. The **throw** with no operand **rethrows** the original exception.

For example:

```
catch(int)
{
    // ...
}
catch(...)   {   // catch everything
    // general error-handling code
    throw;   // rethrow the exception
}
```

In the example just given, if a function **throws** an exception with an **int**, the **catch(...)** handler catches it. That hander performs whatever code is common to all exceptions and then **rethrows** the exception to its specific handler.

Uncaught Exceptions

An uncaught exception is one for which there is no **catch** handler specified or one thrown by a destructor that is executing as the result of another **throw**. Such an exception causes the **terminate** function to be called. You can specify a function for terminate to call by calling the **set_terminate** function, which returns its current value. If no **set_terminate** function call has been made, **terminate** calls **abort**.

Selecting Among *Thrown* Exceptions

To review: A **try** block is followed by one or more **catch** handlers, which are distinguished by their parameter lists. You must decide in your design how to differentiate the exceptions. You might code only one **catch** handler with an **int** parameter and let the value of the parameter determine the **error** type. This approach, illustrated next, assumes that you have control of all of the **throws** in all of the functions in all of the libraries that you use.

```
catch(int exception_code)
{
    switch (exception_code)    {
        case 0:
            // process code 0
            break;
        case 1:
            // process code 1
            break;
        // ....
    }
}
```

No doubt conventions will emerge. One possibility uses class definitions to distinguish exceptions and categories of exceptions. A **throw** with a publicly derived class as its parameter is caught by a **catch** handler with the base class as its parameter. Consider this example:

```
class FileError {
public:
    virtual void HandleException() = 0;
};
class Locked : public FileError {
public:
    void HandleException();
};
class NotFound : public FileError {
public:
    void HandleException();
};

void bar()
```

(continued)

```
{
    try   {
        foo();
    }
    catch(FileError& fe)    {
        fe.HandleException();
    }
}

void foo()
{
    // ...
    if (file_locked)
        throw Locked();
}
```

FileError is a public virtual base class. Its derived classes are **NotFound** and **Locked**. The only **catch** handler for this category of exception is the one with the **FileError** reference parameter. It does not know which of the exceptions was thrown, but it calls the **HandleException** pure virtual function, which automatically calls the proper function in the derived class.

This approach is only one of many that you can use. Instead of classes, you can use enumerated types and have switches in the **catch** handlers. Publishers of libraries will document the conventions that they use to **throw** exceptions, and your **catch** handlers will use those conventions, perhaps using several different conventions in one application. Eventually standards will emerge.

Exceptions and Unreleased Resources

Recall the discussion at the beginning of this chapter about the **setjmp/longjmp** anomaly with unreleased resources. C++ exception handling does not solve that problem. Consider this condition:

```
void foo()
{
    String *str = new String("Hello, Dolly");
    // ...
    if (file_locked)
        throw Locked();
    delete str;
}
```

The **String** object is allocated from the heap by the **new** operator. If the exception is **thrown**, the **delete** operation is not performed. In this case, there are two complications. The memory allocated on the heap for the **String** object is not released, and its destructor is not called, which means that the memory that its constructor allocated for the string value is lost as well.

The same problem exists with dangling open file handles, unclosed screen windows, and other such system resources. If the program just shown seems easy to fix, remember that the **throw** could occur from within a library function far into a stack of nested function calls.

Programming idioms have been suggested that address this problem. Certainly a programmer must consider some of them. Dr. Stroustrup suggests that all such resources can be managed from within automatic instances of resource-management classes. Their destructors would release everything as the **throw** unwinds the stack. Another approach is to make all dynamic heap pointers and file and window handles global so that the **catch** handler could clean everything up. These methods sound cumbersome, however, and they work only if all of the functions in all of the libraries cooperate.

Summary

Exception handling is still being considered by the ANSI X3J16 committee and is still mostly experimental. Although the AT&T specification is the baseline for ANSI standardization, it is very likely that some changes will come about after review by numbers of C++ programmers and compiler developers. When at last you have a compiler that implements exception handling, you should compare its specification with what you have learned in this chapter.

C++ is under your belt now. You know enough about C++ to begin working with it in earnest. Many of you will use one of the compilers in the Appendix. C++ is new enough that no two compilers are the same, even those that are ports of the AT&T licensed version. The programs in this book are as close as possible to all of the implementations. Some of them do not compile with all of the compilers, but the **warnings** and **error** messages will tell you what to change to make the code compatible with your compiler.

You should begin reading about, experimenting with, and learning about object oriented-programming now. Your new knowledge of C++ gives you the tools to build complex object-oriented systems, and that combination will be the programming platform of choice in the decade to come. Chapter 13 applies your new knowledge of C++ to the concepts of object-oriented programming.

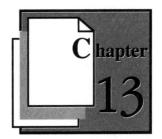

Chapter 13

An Introduction to Object-Oriented Programming

This chapter originally appeared in slightly different form in an earlier book, *C++ Database Development*, by the same author and published by MIS:Press in 1992. The book you are reading now includes the discussion so that you, the new C++ programmer, can associate what you have learned about the C++ language with the terms and concepts of object-oriented programming. You will learn about:

- The differences between procedural and object-oriented programming
- The four characteristics of an object-oriented program
- What an object is
- Abstraction
- Encapsulation
- Methods and messages
- Inheritance
- Polymorphism

331

Many software development languages and environments use the object-oriented programming paradigm as their basis. C++ is the basis for many of them. For example, C++ is at the foundation of what has come to be called *applications frameworks*, which are integrated software development environments that support a particular operating platform, usually a graphical user interface. Microsoft Windows on the PC and X-Windows on UNIX systems are examples of such platforms. These applications frameworks use C++ class libraries to encapsulate the interface and implementation of the operating platform's *applications program interface (API)*. To effectively use one of these software development systems, you must understand not only the characteristics of the C++ language but the object-oriented concepts that underpin the foundations. To build an effective application on top of one of these foundations, you should understand object-oriented design and programming.

As pervasive as object-oriented programming has become, many programmers still do not understand it. By using the exercises in this book you have acquired a working knowledge of C++. That experience alone has exposed you to the object-oriented paradigm without emphasizing it. Having built and used C++ classes, you have already written some object-oriented programs. There are, however, many terms in the object-oriented lexicon that this book has intentionally postponed until this discussion. Simply writing a C++ program does not qualify a programmer as an expert on object-oriented technology. There are rules and procedures to follow, and there are benefits to be gained by understanding and following the disciplines.

The traditional procedure-oriented programmer does not intuitively understand object-oriented programming. The notations and approaches to design are different than what you learned and used in the past. Furthermore, explanations such as the one in this chapter do not usually complete the understanding of object-oriented programming. You need reinforcement—both from experience and by a feeling that there is something to be gained from a new and different approach. Programmers might understand the concepts at the intellectual level and yet not accept them as a pragmatic approach to programming simply because they have been writing good programs all along and see no compelling reason to tamper with that success. For this reason, it is difficult to teach object-oriented programming, although it is not difficult to learn. Learning object-oriented programming is a process of discovery. Teaching it, therefore, becomes the management of that process.

Many of the current generation of programmers have learned and accepted object-oriented programming as a better way to express software algorithms.

Most of them started from the procedural paradigm, having programmed in traditional languages such as C. Those who make the switch become object-oriented advocates. Enough of them have done so that the rest of us cannot deny that there is something to it. You can take a lesson from the observation that once a programmer takes the plunge, he or she almost always becomes a convert. Therefore, the best way to learn object-oriented programming is to try it. Until recently, however, the tools were not widely available. Now, virtually every PC can have a C++ compiler, and virtually every programmer has access to the tools.

The Basics

The first understanding of object-oriented programming is to be found in this design guideline:

The expression of an algorithm should model the application domain that it supports.

This concept reflects an older one that states that the solution to a problem should resemble the problem, a guideline that allows observers of a solution to recognize its purpose without necessarily knowing in advance about the problem. When you see a properly designed word processor, you intuitively understand that the problem being solved is one of capturing and manipulating text. When you see a properly designed inventory management system, you recognize that its purpose is to maintain stock quantities and locations. You recognize those things because the designs resemble and therefore remind you of the problems that they solve.

Carrying this concept to a higher level of abstraction, you recognize that the purpose of a programming language is to express with algorithms the solution to a data processing problem. The techniques used in that expression determine how successfully the solution models its problem domain. Object-oriented programming is one of several different approaches to the expression of algorithms, and it is often misunderstood—primarily by those who do not use it.

Procedural Programming

In the classic approach to programming a programmer designs a set of data structures followed by functions and procedures to process the data. This approach is called *procedural programming* because it starts with the procedures. We are think of programming in this way because that is how programming has been done for forty years.

Procedural programming does not always deliver a solution that resembles the problem, however, because it emphasizes the functions rather than the data—the procedures rather than the objects. Furthermore, procedural programming does not encourage the programmer to separate and hide the procedures related to different data objects from one another. Programmers have long known that those are worthwhile practices, but most procedural programming languages do not encourage them.

Object-Oriented Programming

The world and its applications are not organized into values and procedures separate from one another. Problem solvers in other crafts do not perceive the world that way. They deal with their problem domains by concentrating on the objects and letting the characteristics of those objects determine the procedures to apply to them. To build a house, grow a tomato, or repair a carburetor, first you think about the object and its purpose and behavior. Then you select your tools and procedures. The solution fits the problem.

The world is, therefore, object oriented, and the object-oriented programming paradigm expresses computer programs in ways that model how people perceive the world. Since programmers are people, it is only natural that your approach to the work of the world reflects your view of the world itself. We have not, however, universally learned how to do that. The crafts of carpentry, farming, and mechanics are centuries old, beginning with cultures that lacked technology. The objects and objectives of those trades were understood long before the development of the technologies that support them. Computer programming is relatively new. We are still forming its disciplines, and the technologies are developing faster than we can adjust.

The Object-Oriented Program

An object-oriented program has four fundamental characteristics:

- Abstraction defines new data types.
- Encapsulation designs a data type's representation and its behavior in one encapsulated entity.

- Inheritance derives a new data type from an existing one.
- Polymorphism customizes the behavior of a derived data type.

Object-oriented programming uses a vocabulary of such terms in ways unfamiliar to the procedural programmer. You hear these terms used frequently in discussions of object-oriented programming. Here is a more comprehensive list of object-oriented terms:

abstract base class

abstract data type

abstraction

base class

class

derived class

encapsulation

implementation and interface

inheritance

instantiate

message

method

multiple inheritance

object

polymorphism

subclass

superclass

Now let's use some of those terms. The object-oriented programmer defines an abstract data type by encapsulating its implementation and interface into a class. Inherited abstract data types are derived subclasses of base classes. Within the program the programmer instantiates objects of classes and sends messages to the objects by using the class's methods.

Confused? Don't be concerned; it all makes sense soon enough. The object-oriented programming community uses these terms universally. Therefore, when object-oriented programmers say "encapsulate," for example, you know that their meaning is consistent with the way others use it. When programmers acknowledge that a program is "object oriented," you know that the program contains abstraction, encapsulation, inheritance, and polymorphism, and that it defines abstract data types, instantiates objects, and sends messages to the object's methods. The discussion that follows draws on your experience with C++ to explain these terms.

The Object

The first question that most programmers ask is, "What are the objects in object-oriented programming?" The second question is, "What should be the objects in my design?" These questions reflect this more revealing one: What is it about object-oriented programming that sets it apart from and makes it better than traditional procedural programming? Early writings on the subject effectively explained object-oriented programming to those who already understood it, but their explanations were sometimes too abstruse for a newcomer to fathom, and they did not always justify the paradigm as an improved way to express algorithms.

Simply stated, an object is an instance of a data type. The program in Figure 13.1. declares two objects. The first object is a simple integer; the second object is an abstract data type.

```
void f()
{
    int ndays; // an instance of an int
    Date cdt;  // an instance of an ADT
    // ...
}
```

Figure 13.1 A Program with Two Objects.

Throughout this book you have been declaring objects—instances of the classes that you designed in the exercises. In your prior experience with C and other languages you declared objects when you declared variables. So, what are the objects? They are the variables that you declare. What should be the objects in your object-oriented design? Anything that you build as a class is going to be the data type of an object.

Abstraction

Abstraction is the definition of an abstract data type, which includes the data type's representation and behavior. An abstract data type is a new type. It is not one of the primitive data types that are built into the programming language. The **int**, **long**, and **float** data types are primitive C++ data types. Their data representations and behavior are known to the compiler. For example, an integer data type's format—its representation—and response to arithmetic, assignment, and relational operators—its behavior—are defined as a part of the C++ language.

An abstract data type, however, is not known to the language; the C++ programmer defines the type's format and behavior in a class. For example, the calendar date class used in some of the exercises in earlier chapters is an abstract data type. The compiler and the computer do not know about calendar dates. Programmers have always had to define the behavior of dates by designing structures and functions or by using functions in libraries. The standard C library has several such date definitions, but they are functions and structures, not classes. When you define a C++ calendar date class like the one in Figure 13.2, you express its format and behavior in one design entity. It has **month**, **day**, and **year** data members. It might even support arithmetic and relational operations.

```
class Date  {
    int month, day, year;
public:
    Date(int mo, int da, int yr);
    int operator+(int n);
    // ...
};
```

Figure 13.2 An Abstract Data Type (ADT).

You can then declare an object that has the type of the date class and add to the object, subtract from it, compare it with other objects, assign it to other date objects, and assign values to it. A C++ program declares instances of abstract data types the same way it declares instances of primitive data types. Refer again to Figure 13.1. The declaration of the **cdt** object is an instance of an abstract data type.

C++ programmers often use string classes to implement a string abstract data type similar to the strings of the Basic programming language. The companion diskette with this book includes a string class for you to study. Other abstract data types might be container classes for stacks, lists, trees, and queues, perhaps with ordered and random access variants of such containers. Compiler products often include such container classes in their class libraries.

The term *instantiate* is used by object-oriented programmers for convenience. When an object-oriented program declares an instance of a data type, the program has instantiated an object, whether the data type is primitive or abstract. The program in Figure 13.1 instantiates the **ndays** and **cdt** objects.

Encapsulation

If abstraction is the definition of a C++ class, then encapsulation is its design. A programmer encapsulates the data representation and behavior of an abstract data type into a class, giving it its own implementation and interface. An encapsulated design hides its implementation from the class user and reveals its interface. Figure 13.3 is an example of an encapsulated class.

```
class Date   {
// --- the class implementation
private:
    int month, day, year;
// --- the class interface
public:
    Date(int mo, int da, int yr);
    Date operator+(int n);
    // ...
};
```

Figure 13.3 Encapsulation.

The implementation of a class, which consists of the **private** data members and **private** member functions, is essentially hidden from the using program. The **month, day,** and **year** data members in Figure 13.3 are the class's implementation. A user of the class does not care about the details of implementation—only that it works. The class designer could totally change the implementation—perhaps changing the date representation to a long integer count of days—and the using programs would be unaffected.

The interface, which is visible to the user of the class, consists of the public member functions. The class user reads and modifies values in the data representation by calling **public** member functions. The class interface in Figure 13.3 consists of the constructor, which contains initialization parameters, and an overloaded plus operator, which presumably allows the user of the class to add an integral number of days to the date.

To use the abstract data type defined in Figure 13.3, a programmer makes assumptions about the interface based on its appearance and the programmer's understanding of C++ syntax. If the programmer is not the class's author, those assumptions could be invalid if the class interface design is not intuitive. In the case of Figure 13.3, most programmers would assume that the overloaded plus operator adds an integer to a **Date** object and returns another **Date** object with the result. Figure 13.4 illustrates how the class interface should work.

```
void f()
{
    Date dt(6,29,92);
    dt = dt + 30;   // should now be 7/29/92
}
```

Figure 13.4 An Intuitive Class Interface.

Designing an intuitive class interface is not automatic. The C++ language provides the tools for you to do a proper job, but nothing in the language enforces good design. The class author can use unnecessarily clever techniques that obscure the meaning of the interface. An object-oriented design is not a good design by default. Experienced C++ programmers generally agree on certain design standards for C++ classes. The data members are usually private and constitute most of the implementation. The interface consists only of member functions that restrict access to the data members. The interface is generic in that it is not bound to any particular implementation. The class author should be able to change the implementation without affecting the using programs. These apparent rules are only guidelines, however. Sometimes you need to step around them to achieve some purpose. The fewer times you do that, the stronger your design.

Methods and Messages

Method is another name for C++ public member functions. Methods may be constructors, destructors, procedures, and overloaded operators. They define the class interface. The constructor and overloaded plus operator in Figure 13.3 are methods.

A message is the invocation of a method, which, in C++, is the same thing as calling the public member function. The program sends a message to an object telling it to invoke the method and sometimes provides parameters for the method to use.

There are different kinds of methods characterized by how they support the class definition. There are functional methods, data type methods, and implicit conversion methods. Note that this delineation and these terms are coined here for convenience and are not part of the official object-oriented lexicon. They define different levels of support that C++ provides for class design.

Functional Methods

Figure 13.5 shows three methods added to the **Date** class.

```
class Date  {
    // ...
public:
    // ...
    void Display();         // display the date
    void AdjustMonth(int m); // +/- m months
    int DayOfWeek();        // return 0-6 = Sun-Sat
};
```

Figure 13.5 Functional Methods.

The three methods in Figure 13.5 illustrate three typical method variants. The first method tells the object to do something, in this case, to display itself. The class's implementation knows how to display the object's data representation. The programmer who uses the class is unconcerned about the details of the implementation.

The second method tells the object to change itself, in this case, to adjust its month data value up or down by the integer argument in the method's parameter. This method is an example of one that includes a parameter. Once again, the programmer who uses the class does not care how the object stores the month value or what algorithm adjusts the month, only that it works.

The third method is one that returns a value, in this case, the day of the week represented by the object's current value.

The methods in Figure 13.5 define behavior related to the functional properties of the class. The class is a calendar date, and you want it to behave like a date.

Data Type Methods

Data type methods make a class act like a primitive data type by giving it the properties similar to those of a primitive data type. These properties are usually implemented as overloaded operators in the class interface. Figure 13.5 shows methods that compare dates, assign them to one another, and do some arithmetic on them.

```
class Date   {
    // ...
public:
    // ...
    // ---- arithmetic operators
    Date operator+(int n);
    Date operator-(int n);
    int operator-(Date &dt);
    // ---- assignment operators
    Date& operator=(Date &dt);
```

Figure 13.6 Data Type Methods.

```
     // ---- relational operators
     int operator==(Date &dt);
     int operator!=(Date &dt);
     int operator<(Date &dt);
     int operator>(Date &dt);
};
```

Figure 13.6 Data Type Methods (continued).

Implicit Conversion Methods

The C++ language handles implicit conversion of primitive data types. If you write an expression with an **int** where the compiler expects a **long**, the compiler knows how to make the conversion and does so quietly. If, however, you write an expression where the compiler expects an abstract data type, and you provide a different data type, primitive or abstract, the compiler does not know how to deal with that. Similarly, if the expression expects a primitive data type, and you use an abstract data type, the compiler does not know what to do. In either case, unless you have provided implicit conversion methods, the compiler issues an error message and refuses to compile the program.

You can add implicit conversion methods to a class so that the compiler knows how to convert from one data type to another. The conversion constructor function converts a data type to an abstract data type, and the member conversion function converts an abstract data type to a primitive C++ data type. When you code an expression where the compiler expects to see something other than what you provide as just described, the compiler executes one of your implicit conversion methods to convert the data type. This is an example of a method that you do not explicitly call (or send a message to) from within your program. It executes as the result of the implicit call inferred by the compiler by its interpretation of your expression. Your program implies a call to the method by the context in which it uses data types in an expression.

Figure 13.7 shows two implicit conversion methods added to the **Date** class. The first method converts an **int** data type to a **Date** object. The second method converts a **Date** data type to an **int** object. The conversions are not restricted to converting between abstract data types and primitive data types. You can convert between different abstract data types in the same manner. For example, you might have a **Date** class and a **JulianDate** class, and the same principles apply.

```
class Date  {
    // ...
public:
    // ...
    Date(int n);     // conversion constructor
    operator int(); // member conversion function
};
```

Figure 13.7 Implicit Conversion Methods.

Member Functions

Having just learned about methods and messages in this much detail, you soon find that the terms themselves are not used much in C++ circles. The terms come from the object-oriented lexicon and reflect the syntax of pure object-oriented programming languages such as **SmallTalk**. Most C++ programmers prefer to say that they call member functions rather than send messages through methods, essentially the same thing. Nonetheless, you should understand the analogy, because you will encounter the object-oriented terms.

Inheritance

A class can inherit the characteristics of another class. The original class is called the base class and the new class is called the derived class. You also hear these classes called the *superclass* and the *subclass*. The word *subclass* is also used as a verb to mean the act of inheriting.

The derived class inherits the data representation and behavior of the base class except where the derived class modifies the behavior by overloading member functions. The derived class adds behavior that is unique to its own purpose.

A program can instantiate objects of a base class as well as those of a derived class. If the base class is an abstract base class—one that exists only to be derived from—the program may not instantiate objects of the base class.

Inheritance is the foundation of most object-oriented designs, and it is often overapplied. Some programmers get carried away with the power of inheritance, and C++ can offer some surprises to the unwary designer. Many designs use inheritance to solve problems that would better supported by a different approach, usually an object member of the base class in what is otherwise the derived class. Despite this warning, inheritance is a powerful feature, which, properly used, offers a rich design capability to the object-oriented programmer.

Single Inheritance

The C++ inheritance mechanism lets you build an orderly hierarchy of classes. When several of your abstract data types have characteristics in common, you can design their commonalities into a single base class and separate their unique characteristics into unique derived classes. That is the purpose of inheritance.

For example, a personnel system maintains information about employees. Employees are people, and people have common characteristics—name, address, date of birth, and so on—yet the system might record different kinds of employees. Managers, project workers, and support personnel might be recorded differently. Therefore, you could design a base class of employees that stores name, address, social security number, and date of birth, and then derive separate classes for managers, project workers, and support personnel. Each of the derived classes would inherit the characteristics of the **employee** class and would have additional characteristics common to themselves. For example, the **manager** class might include an annual salary-augmenting bonus data member that the other **employee** classes do not have. The **project worker** class could have a list of project assignments. The **support personnel** class could record overtime hours worked.

Object-oriented designers strive to use inheritance to model relationships where the derived class "is a kind of" the base class. A car "is a kind of" vehicle. An engineer "is a kind of" employee, which "is a kind of" person. This relationship is called the **ISA** relationship. Inheritance is not appropriate for relationships where one class has an instance of another. An employee "has a" date of birth. A department "has a" manager. This relationship is called the **HASA** relationship. Instead of using inheritance, the class that "has" an object of another class embeds the object as a data member.

Multiple Inheritance

A derived class can inherit the characteristics of more than one base class. This technique is called *multiple inheritance*. Not all object-oriented programming languages support multiple inheritance, and many experts assert that it is not a necessary design tool. Nonetheless, C++ does support multiple inheritance, and there are times when you find it a good way to express class relationships.

You recall that the effectiveness of a programming language can be measured in its ability to model the problem domains that it supports. The objects in the world reflect membership in multiple-inheritance hierarchies, and programmers are called upon to write programs to model those objects. A sofabed is a sofa and it is a bed, both of which are items of furniture. An amphibious airplane is a boat and an airplane, both of which are vehicles. A carphone is not a car and a telephone, however, and sometimes programmers get their designs confused by thinking that they need to inherit when they do not.

Suppose that the system supported by the class design just discussed needed to store the **support personnel** class as an entry in a linked list. The **support person** class "is a kind of" employee, and now it "is a kind of" linked list entry, too. The other employees are not listed in that manner, so their classes do not need to inherit the characteristics of the linked list. You might argue that in life a person is not a linked list entry and that this solution does not clearly model the real-world problem. That argument would depend on what the linked list does and who is reading the design. If the linked list is a convenient way to represent the employee's seniority ranking in a union membership, for example, then the relationship is valid because the employee "is a kind of" union member. That might not be clear to everyone who reads the design documentation, so use notation that clearly describes the purpose for the class relationship. If, on the other hand, you are using the linked list to maintain some arbitrary sort sequence for the **support** class, then perhaps a different design approach would be more appropriate.

Polymorphism

Polymorphism exists when a derived class customizes the behavior of the base class to meet the requirements of the derived class. A C++ base class uses the virtual member function to specify that overriding member functions in derived classes have polymorphic behavior with respect to that method.

If a derived class overrides a base class method, and the base class method is not a virtual function, then the overriding behavior is effective only when the compiler is de-referencing a pointer, reference, or object of the derived class itself. If the object's pointer or reference refers to the base class, then the base class method has precedence. Such behavior is not polymorphic. However, if the base class method is virtual, then the compiler selects the overriding derived class method regardless of the type being de-referenced by the compiler.

Suppose, for example, that the **support staff** class in this discussion was further decomposed into derived classes that represented the various kinds of support personnel. You could have typists, corporate pilots, chauffers, maintenance personnel, instructors, and so on. The system measures skill levels differently for each of these disciplines, yet there is a requirement for a general-purpose skill index for the base support class. Each derived class exhibits different behavior for data entry and retrieval of the skill index, but some parts of the system invoke the skill method without knowing which kind of **support personnel** object is involved. The polymorphic skill method would modify the class's behavior at run-time based on the type of the derived class.

Summary

The object-oriented programming paradigm is a rich environment for the expression of the data formats and functions for an application. It is not necessary, however, for C++ programmers to immerse themselves totally in the object-oriented passion. The availability of improved design and programming methods does not automatically outdate all of the traditional approaches. C++ has the facility to support the basics of object-oriented programming while permitting the programmer to use traditional procedural programming where it seems appropriate. C++, in fact, encourages that approach. By supporting traditional C flow control of nested functions, C++ allows you to leverage your existing investment in mature and useful C function libraries. Furthermore, C++ does not force a pure object-oriented hierarchical data structure where every data type descends from one generic root base object. Instead, C++ allows you to build a number of class hierarchies representing the different problem domains that your application might deal with. There can be classes that define the data structures of the application's functional purpose; there can be classes that supply general-purpose data structures such as strings, lists, queues, and so on; there can be classes that integrate your application with a particular user interface. All these classes can coexist independently of one another in a system of hierarchies integrated by you into an application.

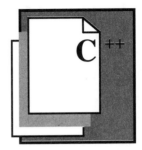

Appendix:
C++ Compilers

This appendix contains a list of C++ compilers that you can use to compile and operate the exercises in this book. The list is not comprehensive, and new products are being introduced all of the time. The exercises are tested with Borland, Comeau, Microsoft, and Zortech C++. The book identifies where there are differences between compilers and where certain exercises do not work with one of those three compilers.

Modifications are possible to the exercises when C++ or the compilers change or for compatibility with compilers not yet tested. The companion diskette will have all such modifications identified and explained.

347

Borland C++ 3.1

Borland International, Inc.

1800 Green Hills Road

PO Box 660001

Scotts Valley, CA 95066-0001

(408) 438-5300

Borland C++ is a compiler implementation of C++ that runs on MS-DOS and OS/2 systems. It is the descendent of the very popular Turbo C. Borland C++ comes in many configurations supporting OS/2, Windows, and DOS development and target environments.

Comeau C++ 3.0

Comeau Computing

91-34 120th Street

Richmond Hill, NY 11418

(718) 945-0009

Comeau C++ is a CFRONT port, which means that it is an adaptation of the AT&T C++ translator to run under MS-DOS and UNIX. The CFRONT program reads your C++ source code and translates it into C code, which must be compiled by a C compiler. You need a C compiler to compile the translated output from Comeau C++. The MS-DOS version uses Microsoft C. Developers who want guaranteed CFRONT-compatible code for developing on MS-DOS and other desktop platforms to port to UNIX targets will find Comeau C++ a good choice.

Computer Innovations C++

Computer Innovations, Inc.

980 Shrewsbury Avenue

Tinton Falls, NJ 07724-3003

(908) 542-5920

Computer Innovations C++ is a UNIX implementation of CFRONT that runs on 386/486 UNIX systems. It includes a copy of this book to help programmers get started.

Microsoft C++ 8.0

One Microsoft Way

Redmond, WA 98052

Microsoft added the 8.0 designation to their C/C++ version 7.0 compiler when they introduced the Visual C++ Windows development environment. The C++ compiler is actually Version One for Microsoft, having been introduced in 1992. Earlier versions of the compiler supported the C language only. Microsoft C++ does not support templates. Its support for exception handling is managed by a macro emulation that is not the exception handling package specified by AT&T. It is, however, the only exception handling package available on MS-DOS compilers.

Zortech C++ 3.1

Symantec Corporation

10201 Torre Avenue

Cupertino, CA 95014

(408) 253-9600

The Zortech compiler was the first of the C++ compilers for MS-DOS systems. For a long time Zortech went in their own directions with their implementation and interpretation of how C++ should work. Recent versions, however, have moved closer to the AT&T specification. Depending on when you got the compiler, you might need to get some patches from Symantec for all of the exercises in this book to work. Specifically, get an updated copy of **iomanip.h** if the exercises with the **setw** manipulator do not work correctly. Some of the template exercises do not work with Zortech C++.

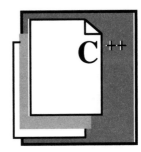

Glossary

This glossary defines C++ and object-oriented programming terms.

abstract base class   A class definition which is always a base class for other classes to be derived from. No specific objects of the base class are declared by the program. A C++ abstract base classes is one that has a pure virtual function, a protected constructor, or a protected destructor.

abstract data type   Also called ADT. A user-defined data type built as a C++ class. The details of implementation are not necessarily a part of the ADT. See also primitive data type and concrete data type.

abstraction   Defining an abstract data type by designing a class.

anonomous object   An internal, temporary object created by the compiler.

argument	The value passed to a function. Its type must match that of the function's corresponding parameter as declared in the function's prototype. See "parameter."
base class	A class from which other classes derive characteristics. All the characteristics of the base are inherited by the derived class. Also called *superclass*.
class	A user-defined data type that may consist of data members and member functions.
class hierarchy	A system of base and derived classes.
concrete data type	A user-defined or library data type complete with interface and implementation. The CDT is meant to be instantiated as an object and is not intended solely to be derived from.
constructor	The function executed by the compiler when the program declares an instance of a class. See also "destructor".
data member	A data component of a class. It may be any valid data type including class objects and references.
declaration	As opposed to definition. A declaration is the statement that declares the existence of an object. A declaration reserves memory.
definition	As opposed to declaration. A definition is the statement that defines the format of a type. A definition reserves no memory.
derived class	A class that inherits some of its characteristics from a base class. Also called a *subclass*.

destructor	The function executed by the compiler when a declared instance of a class goes out of scope. See also "constructor."
encapsulation	The activity of defining a class with its data members and member functions encapsulated into the definition. Encapsulation implies an implementation, which is hidden from the class user, and an interface, which is visible to the class user.
extraction operator	The overloaded >> operator that reads (extracts) values from an input stream. See also "insertion operator."
free store	The C++ heap. A dynamic memory pool that programs use to allocate and release temporary memory buffers.
friend	A class or function that has access to the private members of a class but that is not a member of that class. The class definition declares the **friend**.
hierarchy	See "class hierarchy."
inheritance	The ability for one class to inherit the characteristics of another. The inherited class is said to be derived from the base class. Also called *subclassing*.
implementation	The private members of a class. The implementation defines the details of how the class implements the behavior of the abstract base type. See also "interface."
inline function	A function that the compiler compiles as in-line code every time the function is called.

insertion operator

The overloaded << operator that writes (inserts) values to an output stream. See also "extraction operator."

instantiate

Declare an object of a data type, usually a class.

interface

The public members of a class, which define the class user's interface to the class's data and its behavior. Usually implemented as member functions. See also "implementation."

intrinsic data type

See "primitive data type."

linkage specification

Notation that tells the C++ compiler that a function was or is to be compiled with the linkage conventions of another language.

manipulator

A value that a program sends to a stream to tell the stream to modify one of its modes.

member

A component of a class, either a data member or a member function.

member function

A function component of a class, also called a *method*. A member function may be virtual.

message

A message is the invocation of a class's member function in the name of a declared object of the class. The message is said to be sent to the object to tell it to perform its function. The message includes the function call and the arguments that accompany it.

method

A method in C++ is a member function of a class. Programs send messages to objects by invoking methods.

multiple inheritance	The ability for a derived class to inherit the characteristics of more than one base class.
object	A declared instance of a data type including standard C++ data types as well as objects of classes.
object database	A collection of persistent objects.
overloaded function	A function that has the same name as one or more other functions but that has a different parameter list. The compiler selects which function to call based on the data types and number of arguments in the call.
overloaded operator	A function that executes when a C++ operator is seen in a defined context with respect to a class object.
overriding function	A function in a derived class that has the same name, return type, and parameter list as a function in the base class. The compiler calls the **overriding** function when the program calls that function in the name of an object of the derived class. If the function in the base class is virtual, the compiler calls the derived class's function even when the call is through a pointer or reference to the base class. See also "pure virtual function."
parameter	The declaration of a data item that a function expects to be passed to it. This declaration includes the item's type and name and appears in the function's declaration block at the beginning of the function. When the parameter appears in the function's prototype, the parameter's name may be omitted. See "argument" and "prototype."

parameter list	The list of parameter types and names in a function declaration block. Also the same list, which may exclude the names, in a function prototype.
persistence	The ability of an object to succeed its creator and to subsequently exist in space other than the space in which it was created.
persistent object	An object that exhibits persistence.
polymorphism	The ability for methods in a class hierarchy to exhibit different behavior for the same message depending on the type of the object for which the method is invoked and without regard to the class type of the reference to the object.
primitive data type	A data type known to the compiler. Primitive data types in C++ are **char**, **int**, **float**, **double**, and **pointer**. The integer types may be further qualified as **long**, **short**, and **unsigned**. All types may be organized into arrays of like types and structures and unions of varying types. Also called *intrinsic data types*.
private class members	Members of a class for which access is granted only to the class's member functions and to **friend** functions of the class.
protected class members	Members of a class that are private except to member functions of derived classes.
prototype	The definition of a function's name, return type, and parameter list.
public class members	Members of a class to which access is granted to all functions within the scope of an object of the class.

pure virtual function A virtual function in a base class that must have a matching function in a derived class. A program may not declare an instance of a class that has a pure virtual function. A program may not declare an instance of a derived class if that derived class has not provided an overriding function for each pure virtual function in the base.

reference A variable name that is an alias for another variable.

stream A category of character-oriented data files or devices where the data characters exist in an input or output stream.

subclass See "derived class."

subclassing See "inheritance."

superclass See "base class."

this A pointer that exists in all nonstatic member functions. The pointer is a pointer to an object of the class. It points to the object for which the function is being executed.

type The type of a program constant or variable, which can be of a primitive or an abstract data type.

type conversion The conversion of one type to another. The compiler has built-in type conversions, and a class may define its own conversions for converting from an object of the class to another type and from another type to an object of the class.

type-safe linkage

A technique that insures that functions and function calls in separately compiled program modules use consistent parameter lists.

virtual function

A member function in a class from which other classes may be derived. If the derived class has a function with the same name and parameter list, the derived class's function is always executed for objects of the derived class. See also "pure virtual function" and "overriding function."

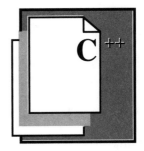

Bibliography

Following is a list of the articles, books, and publications that contributed to the research for *teach yourself... C++*.

AT&T *Library Manual*, C++ Stream Library, 1989.

AT&T *C++ Reference Manual*, 1989.

Cantu, Marco, and Tendon, Steve, *Borland C++ 3.1 Object-Oriented Programming*, 1992, Bantam Computer Books.

Cargill, Tom, *C++ Programming Style*, 1992, Addison-Wesley.

Coplien, James O., *Advanced C++ Programming Styles and Idioms*, 1992, Addison-Wesley.

Dewhurst, Stephen C., and Stark, Kathy T., *Programming in C++*, 1989, Prentice Hall.

Dlugosz, John M., *Computer Language Magazine*, August 1988, The Secret of Reference Variables.

Ellis, Margaret A., and Stroustrup, Bjarne, *The Annotated C++ Reference Manual*, 1990, Addison-Wesley.

Lippman, Stanley B., *C++ Primer*, 1989, Addison-Wesley.

Murray, Robert B., *C++ Strategies and Tactics*, 1993, Addison-Wesley.

Myers, Scott, *Effective C++*, Addison-Wesley.

Pohl, Ira, *C++ for C Programmers*, 1989, The Benjamin/Cummings Publishing Company, Inc.

Stevens, Al, *C++ Database Development*, 1992, MIS:Press.

Stroustrup, Bjarne, *The C++ Programming Language*, 2nd Ed., 1991, Addison-Wesley.

Wiener, Richard S., and Pinson, Lewis J., *An Introduction to Object-Oriented Programming and C++*, 1988, Addison-Wesley.

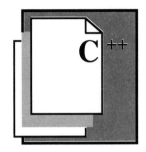

Index